629.28
His

629.28
~~796.7~~
W

Jv.H

Wallach, Theresa

Easy motorcycle riding

DATE DUE				
11-24				
12-18				
8-14				
9-13				
4-9				

easy **MOTORCYCLE** *riding*

The author on a racing bike of the time.

easy MOTORCYCLE *riding*

ENLARGED EDITION

By THERESA WALLACH

Illustrated by Maggie MacGowan

STERLING PUBLISHING CO., INC. NEW YORK
Oak Tree Press Co., Ltd
London & Sydney

STERLING SPORTS BOOKS

Advanced Tennis
Baseball
Basketball
Bike-Ways
Competitive Weightlifting
Fine Points of Tennis
Getting Started in Tennis
Girls' Basketball (Revised)
Girls' Gymnastics
Golf Explained

Handball Basics
Junior Tennis
Marathon: The World of Long-
    Distance Athletes
Start Golf Young (Revised)
Table Tennis
Warm Up for Little League Baseball
Warm Up for Soccer
Wrestling
Yoga for Kids

Soccer the Way the Pros Play

Copyright © 1978, 1970 by Sterling Publishing Co., Inc.
Two Park Avenue, New York, N.Y. 10016
Distributed in Australia and New Zealand by Oak Tree Press Co., Ltd.,
P.O. Box J34, Brickfield Hill, Sydney 2000, N.S.W.
Distributed in the United Kingdom and elsewhere in the British Commonwealth
by Ward Lock Ltd., 116 Baker Street, London W.1
Manufactured in the United States of America
All rights reserved
Library of Congress Catalog Card No.: 78-57787
Sterling ISBN 0-8069-4134-0 Trade   Oak Tree 7061-2591-6
4135-9 Library

CONTENTS

1. Before You Begin 7
2. A Trial Ride 9
3. King of the Road 19
4. Come—Visit with Me 30
5. A Better Understanding 34
6. Getting Acquainted 49
7. The Art of Cornering 58
8. The Foot Gearshift 65
9. Roadcraft 69
10. Advanced Riding 81
11. Dimensional Riding 89
12. What to Wear 96
13. Your First New Motorcycle 101
14. Your First Used Motorcycle 108
15. How to Check a Used Motorcycle . . . 114
    Checklist 114
    1. Accessories 115
    2. Air Filter 116
    3. Alternator 117
    4. Appearance 117
    5. Battery 118
    6. Brakes 119
    7. Cables 120
    8. Carburetor 120
    9. Chains 121
    10. Clutch 122
    11. Contacts 122
    12. Controls and Levers 123
    13. Engine 123
    14. Footrests 124
    15. Frame 125
    16. Front Forks 125

17. Fuel Taps	126
18. Fuse	126
19. Generator	127
20. Guards Shields and Brackets	127
21. Handlebars	127
22. Horn	128
23. Instruments	128
24. License and Documents	129
25. Lights	131
26. Locks and Keys	131
27. Lubrication	132
28. Manual	132
29. Modifications	133
30. Mufflers	133
31. Nuts and Bolts	133
32. Price	134
33. Road Test	135
34. Rubbers	135
35. Seating	135
36. Shock Absorbers Rear Suspension	136
37. Spark Plug	136
38. Spokes	137
39. Sprocket	137
40. Stands	137
41. Steering	138
42. Storage	138
43. Switches	139
44. Technical Data	139
45. Tires	141
46. Tools	142
47. Transmission	142
48. Voltage Regulator	142
49. Wheels	143
50. Wiring	143
16. Professional Instruction	145
Glossary	153
Index	157

1. BEFORE YOU BEGIN

Many people will be encouraged to become better acquainted with motorcycling and enjoy good riding, if they are able to obtain helpful and accurate information. Given this assistance, beginners may safely learn without the fear and danger of getting astride a motorcycle and attempting to teach themselves.

If you want to learn to be a good motorcycle rider and you happen to have a friend who rides, you are probably glad to be together. There is something exciting about motorcycling. Your friend may be an experienced rider, active in a club, or an official at competitive events—one who is largely responsible for encouraging good motorcycling in some way or other.

Most genuine motorcyclists are ready to help. This good will and know-how gives you an opportunity for a good beginning and an excellent introduction to motorcycling. For a beginner this is an ideal as well as a safe way to learn. In addition to getting sound advice and plenty of encouragement—if indeed that should be necessary—you will not be alone with your problems. Riding hints and tips can be discussed with your friend and it is possible for you to learn good style. Whether you debate a road run or a technical topic, club or business meetings, or just "bench-racing," the conversation will give you a chance to learn something before you get on a motorcycle.

Other beginners learn motorcycling by information picked up in places which are anything but reliable. Enthusiasm keeps them going and they seem to survive more by luck and the law of self-preservation than by riding skill. Whatever their talent, that is not the best way to learn to ride. They will never enjoy the full capabilities of themselves or of their machines like those fortunate enough to have had proper instruction. It takes time and effort to understand the motorcycle as a two-wheeled vehicle.

Least fortunate of all are the newcomers who are left entirely to their own resources. They get their experience the hard way. Some admit their mistakes when it is too late.

Naturally you do not want to make the same mistakes or take the same risks. The safest and most sensible way to become a good motorcycle rider is by getting the guidance and information necessary for a true knowledge of the subject.

The new rider, whatever his age, wants one thing above all else: to get astride and ride his motorcycle. He is eager to learn to ride properly, but where can he go to find the right way?

Personal instruction by an expert is the best way, but not every novice is able to attend a course of motorcycle riding instruction. Good reading material can help wherever motorcycles are ridden, particularly where other assistance is not readily available.

This book, then, traces the pathway to correct and easy riding. Never before has the right kind of information reached the beginner in time to prevent an accident for which the motorcycle was not to blame.

This book is written for motorcycle riders everywhere. The aim is to prepare the beginner for a safe learning period and also to bring present owners of motorcycles a little closer to fully understanding their mounts.

2. A TRIAL RIDE

If you have just purchased your first motorcycle, the temptation to begin riding will be irresistible. While you have a great deal to learn before venturing into traffic, this chapter, along with your owner's instruction manual, will enable you to maintain a sense of confidence while you get the "feel" of your machine and master the rudiments of stopping, starting, and turning.

Much can be learned indoors before attempting to ride. Take a few extra moments before going out to become familiar with the controls. Every action must be clear in your mind by the time the engine is started and put into gear so that any response however spontaneous will be a right one. From your owner's manual you will find how to turn on the fuel tap(s) and where to switch on the ignition. Make sure the transmission is in neutral. Depress the kickstarter with your foot and your engine will start. Give yourself time to gain experience and you will have no difficulty starting your engine.

Listen to the engine "speed" or revolutions as you open the twistgrip extremely slowly and remember that what you do with your right hand will also affect the traction spot where your rear (driving) wheel touches the ground. Unless you are testing for some reason, "blipping-the-throttle" serves no good purpose. Sudden opening and shutting of the twistgrip puts an undue strain on the engine whereas twistgrip control means the smooth ability to regulate engine revolutions to a fine degree.

Try your riding position with the machine up on the center-stand. Keep your arms loose and elbows

A TRIAL RIDE

With the motorcycle up on the center-stand, take your riding position, and try steering through the whole range.

bent so you can steer easily through the whole range. Your right foot is your brake foot and your left is the gear-shift foot. Operate the clutch and get the feel of the controls while the back wheel is off the ground so that there will be no risk of errors nor danger of traffic. It is well worthwhile spending time to set the levers correctly. Controls should be easy to reach without delay. Handlebars and footrests should be adjusted so they are naturally comfortable and give you the most suitable riding position. Awkwardly placed levers are difficult to use and tiresome on long journeys. Unless you are at ease and relaxed you will not have the control needed for an awkward situation. The drive to the back wheel is disengaged when in the "neutral" gear position. The clutch lever as the word implies will "clutch" when in the released position. It will "de-clutch" (held-in position) the drive when you are in gear. Feel how much "free play" movement there is in the foot brake pedal. Learn when to expect your

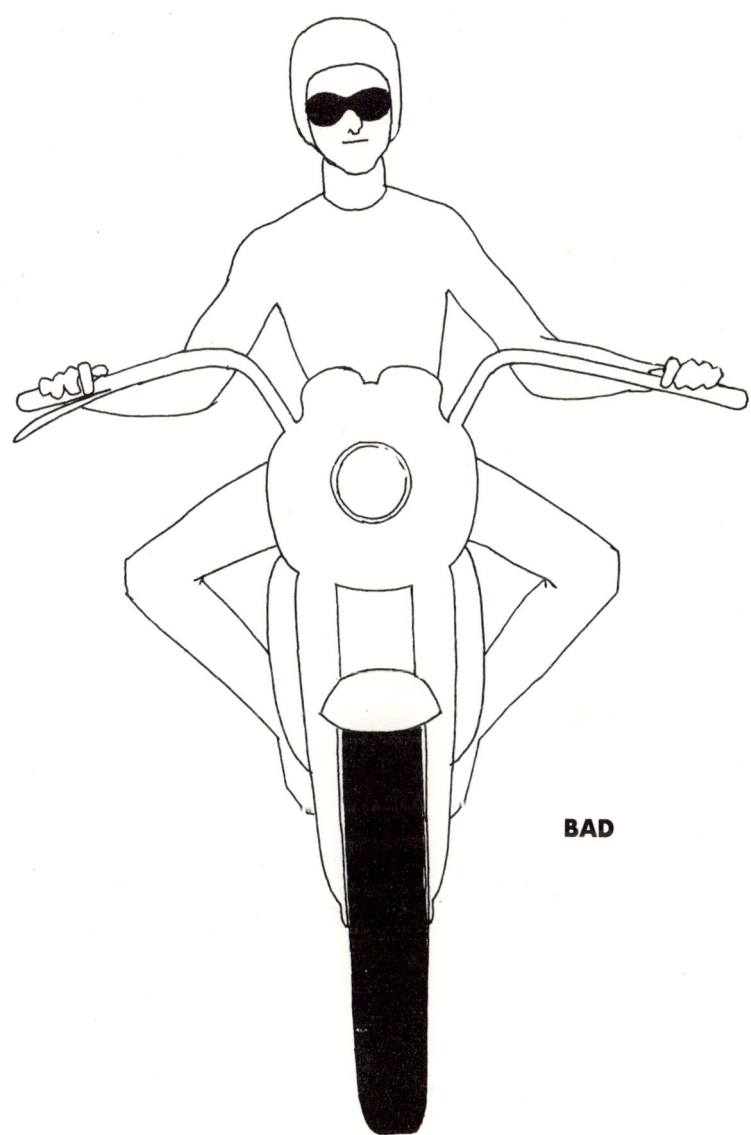

BAD

Never let your knees and thighs splay outward like this. Hug the tank.

back brake to come on with gentle pressure from your toe so you will not skid. The greatest possible part of yourself should be in contact with your mount. Cover the area alongside the fuel tank with knees and thighs and make good use of tank pads or knee grips if rubbers are fitted. Remain in contact with them always. If you expect to be in command of weight distribution, levers, and foot controls at all times, then you must maintain constant contact with them.

As you start your trial ride, remain calm and do not get excited when you feel the power begin to take you along. As explained, the only way to make the correct approach is to start with the rudimentary exercises upon which all your advanced maneuvers will have their foundation.

Learning to move off and to come to a halt should be limited to being under a little power for only a very short time. The distance in between is not the means to the accomplishment. We know very well that the proper place for the feet is not along the ground, but it is too much to expect safe co-ordination between hands and feet (twistgrip-clutch-gearlever-brake) in the beginning. Use your feet for the restrained crawling pace that will be much too slow for normal balance. Equalize your hands first. It takes self-control. You are both the pupil and the teacher in one. If you are entirely alone, the possibility of mechanical damage is as great as the personal risk unless you have some sort of discipline. Turn the machine toward a fence or soft barrier that will stop you without too much damage if you overshoot and roll into it. Pull in (de-clutch) the clutch lever to disengage the drive (transmission). With your left foot put the gear lever into first (bottom) gear. Gradually, gently and very smoothly, open the twistgrip (fuel), while at the same time—even more gently—releasing the clutch lever. Your hands—right on the twistgrip and left on the clutch lever—blend to give your ma-

A TRIAL RIDE

Learn how to move off and use your feet for the restrained crawling pace.

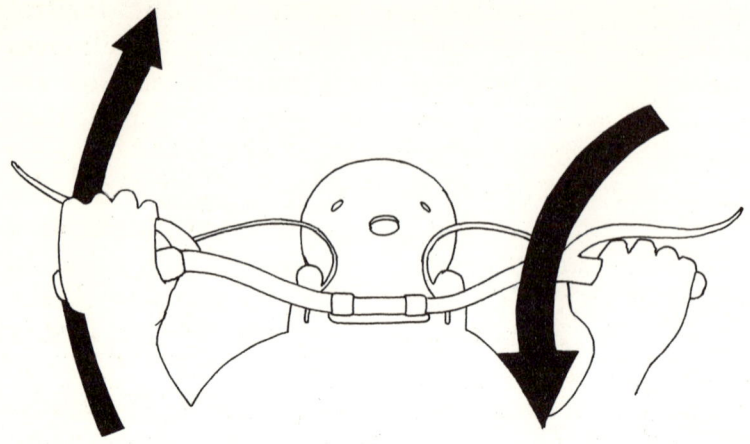

Open the twistgrip (fuel) while at the same time—even more gently—releasing the clutch lever.

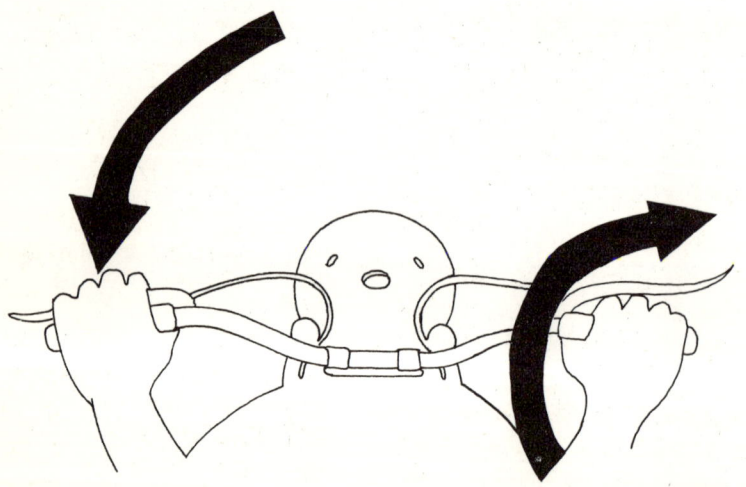

To stop, pull in the clutch lever (de-clutch) and close the twistgrip (no fuel).

chine a balanced diet, and it will move forward smoothly, taking up the load (work).

To stop, pull in (de-clutch) the clutch lever (no work), close the twistgrip (no fuel). Practice moving

A TRIAL RIDE

off gradually and stopping nicely by hand control only. Let your feet hold you up as the machine moves forward only a little way at a time. When you are ready to go a little faster for natural balance, then practice getting your feet up on the footrests as quickly as possible. The more thoroughly you work, the more variations of this exercise you will think of: a left circle and then one in the opposite direction to switch the attitude of your hands. Use the front brake as you close the twistgrip. Take care. The brake says "Stop" and the twistgrip says "Go" and both are in the same hand. Learn to handle your controls fluently. Your capacity to move off must always be matched by the ability to stop.

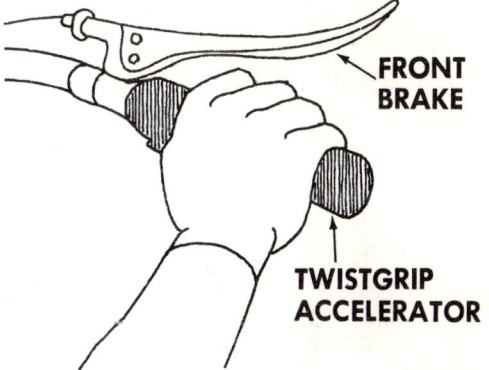

The brake says STOP and the twistgrip says GO. Both are operated by the same hand.

FRONT BRAKE

TWISTGRIP ACCELERATOR

Now for your feet. Start on the most important side. The brake foot will be required with greater urgency than the gear foot. Gear shifting is not so critical, but your brake foot should always be on guard. Practice the same exercise—starting and stopping with only a very short distance in between. Come to a halt using your foot brake. As you stop, your gear foot has to support you. The brake foot is on duty. Be able to come to a halt with equal ease in a right (brake side) or left (gear side) turn. There will be many a time in traffic jams when you will steer or veer to the right and require that ability. Separate your learning into small steps and pay attention to the purpose of each particular maneuver. In other words, understand your problem.

Next, pace your machine through the cross-over point of a small figure-eight being careful to keep the engine revolutions steady regardless of the switch of handlebar direction. Hands must continue to be in accord all through the steering range from one side to the other, and, of course, this cannot be learned when riding fast.

You have a problem already. How to stop and support yourself with the correct foot when in a brake side turn? You must learn to do this. Counteract the imbalance by pushing against the machine with the right knee against the side of the tank and heel it to the gear foot (support) side. The front wheel (steering), providing its direction remains to the right and has not been straightened out ahead, will offer you some support. The trick will be to incline the machine to about twenty degrees over to the left (support) side. As explained earlier, if you expect to be in charge of your rear brake in awkward circumstances then you should at least have your foot on it. When a foot comes away from a control to aid balance by touching the ground, the effectiveness of that control is gone. An off-and-on-the-control foot is unreliable. Prodding along the ground and dragging your feet to balance yourself not only looks silly, but it is unsafe and will spoil much of your pleasure. Your brake foot is obligated to you every moment you are astride the dual-seat whether in motion or stationary. Be ready and able to use that foot brake in a tight corner without getting off balance in the turn. In an emergency this is very likely to happen because a brake-side street corner is just the place where trouble happens. Always stop with the right foot up on the brake pedal and the other (gearshift) foot down on the ground for support. Never the other way around. It takes a little practice to lay the machine over from one side for

A TRIAL RIDE

Always stop with the brake foot (right) up and the gearshift foot (left) down.

"Stop" and switch your feet to the other side for "Go," but it is not difficult.

Once you can be sure that you will not get out of control, lurch forward, or surprise yourself when starting and stopping, then you will be ready to go on. Know the position of your controls and think out your moves in advance so you will not have to look about for the controls and forget to look where you are going. Panic is the result of giving all your attention to one thing. Soon you will have both feet aboard and be riding smoothly around the area. Your machine will at last be evenly balanced. It will handle as it should and even the most timid beginner will have a feeling of confidence. Remain in first (bottom) gear and ride around until you can tell where you belong on the machine and find your true seat. There is more than one way to ride a motorcycle, but fundamentally there is only one correct way to move off and to come to a halt. Proper instruction does not take into consideration a person who says, "Well, I stopped." We are concerned only with a rational way to ride.

Prepare your feet for the role each has to play when you want to come in. While you are out there have your gear foot engage neutral for you and "coast" in to finish. This finds you in the identical position as when you were getting acquainted and mounting the machine at the very beginning. Repeating the position: Brake foot up; gear foot down; and hands free. When you sit astride your stationary machine, the way you are mounted will indicate whether you are "coming in" or whether you are "going off." Understand the purpose for this routine and train yourself to do it well until you become the extension of your mechanical controls. If some bit of advice saves your life only once, it will have been worth learning.

3. KING OF THE ROAD

Motorcycling is a delightful sport besides being a useful means of transportation. You enjoy the smell of springtime, the warmth of summer and the crisp winds of autumn. You may own an iron steed that is more economical than shoe leather and more powerful than the strongest, fastest horse ever bred. The motorcycle is not temperamental. It is perfectly obedient. It will do exactly what it is told to do—climb a curb and mount an embankment to escape danger, or toss you into the gutter. A motorcycle can be the safest vehicle on the road because of its flexibility, or the most dangerous because of its vulnerability. It all depends on the skill of the rider.

This guide for the beginner is the first step toward good motorcycling and it is intended to save lives. The information is based on years of road experience, racing, and competition riding, in addition to teaching beginners and experienced riders to ride better and more safely. Motorcycle instruction may not at first seem to be important, but given the opportunity of a good beginning, it is very effective and does account for the best riders. Some of my pupils never had any intention of having a motorcycle until the idea was put to them in an informative way. More people than ever before are buying motorcycles and taking to the roads and trails on two wheels to enjoy the fresh air and to be independent. None of those who take the trouble to learn to ride well are disappointed.

There is very little educational material available on motorcycling and it is difficult for the beginner to find whatever information might be helpful. Much of the advice that is readily obtainable is in the form of brochures, newspaper stories and magazine articles, and is trivial. Some of the information is wrong and misinformation can be dangerous to a motorcycle rider.

The good motorcyclist is King of the Road. You are on your own. You are not protected by two tons of steel, rubber, foam padding and safety glass. Neither are you steering two tons of guided missile toward other cars, people and property. If you are prepared to accept the responsibility of your own actions, then motorcycling can be both safe and thrilling. Riding is an art as well as a craft and no amount of explanation can take the place of experience.

This does not mean, however, that you should try all sorts of experiments that are only going to lead to trouble. The only correct approach is to start with the rudimentary exercises upon which all your advanced maneuvers will ultimately be built. If you are one of those who has been a little afraid of motorcycles, it is most likely because you never had anybody to explain them. As with most skills, it is easy when you know how. Failure to be completely familiar with the controls and to know their effect under different road conditions is like trying to learn to fly an airplane by trial and error.

Special attention to detail at the beginning is very important. You will be well rewarded when you have learned the main points and practiced on private ground or in a restricted area.

Good results were obtained when older pupils were carefully instructed and who until then, had the mistaken belief that each was too old to ride a motorcycle. Many an elderly person now owns a lightweight to get about on. Physical fitness is not so important in this instance. The trouble lies with the physically fit rider who has not learned good riding. Any intelligent person with the right mental attitude can become a skilled rider, regardless of age, size, or shape. When

The modern motorcycle—spirited and dependable—lets you enjoy the smell of springtime, the warmth of summer and the crisp winds of autumn.

KING OF THE ROAD

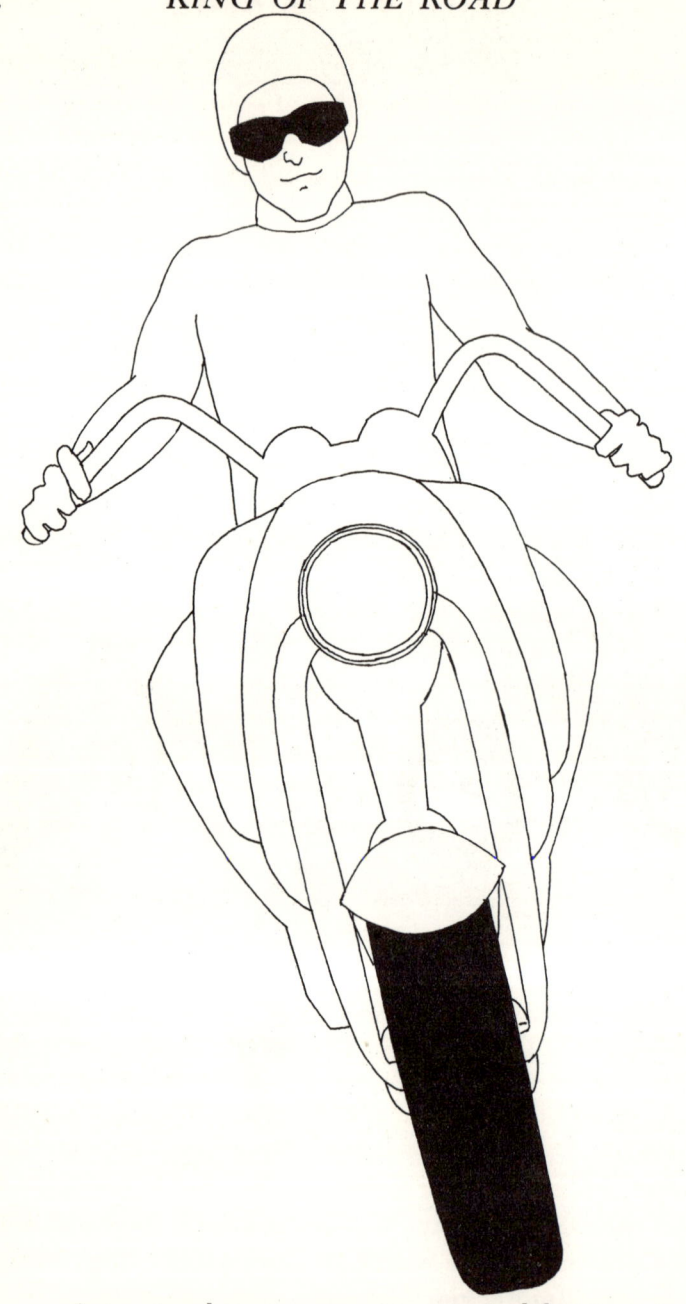

On an iron steed you are not protected by two tons of steel, rubber, foam padding and safety glass.

KING OF THE ROAD

you begin to ride, you will quickly realize how many occasions there are when it is possible to do more on two wheels than in a heavier, more expensive car.

Ways and means to improve the knowledge and skill of the motorcycle rider have not kept pace with the rapid mechanical improvement of the machine. Every other kind of activity has professional instruction readily available. Much assistance is always given to teaching car drivers and to the operation of other types of equipment. Thousands of cars are loaned to driving schools by dealers and sometimes with financial aid from manufacturers.

It is unfortunate such aid is not given to those who would like to learn motorcycling. Especially since, unlike any other vehicle, a motorcycle puts you on your own right from the start. It is the only conveyance in which the learner is entirely alone at the controls. There is nobody with you to see you safely on your way. A companion or instructor is unable to restrain you physically or to reach the controls when you make a mistake and so it is important that you learn to ride by practicing each step after first getting it into your head. Your improving knowledge and skill will bring a better appreciation of those manufacturing advances in what is a beautiful piece of engineering.

The law in different places varies. There are unfortunately many places where any person who is of legal age and has a car driving license may buy a high-power motorcycle, and even carry a passenger along an expressway without ever having been on a motorcycle before. He may qualify for a license by demonstrating his skill at driving on four wheels. Then he will use this license as a permit to operate something quite different: a motorcycle. The authorities should distinguish between driving and riding. A meaningful motorcycle test would help to control cycling, and aid in reducing the accident statistics that prejudice the public against motorcycling.

Good testing and examinations cannot be provided unless these authorities actually have personnel who themselves know what is good riding and preferably are themselves good riders.

Sometimes a person rides who is not in harmony with two wheels. Emotionally some are not suited to the more exacting standard of motorcycle riding and the restraint necessary. Others seem to risk getting into trouble rather than think in advance or find information and seek help of any kind. When there is trouble, these types always blame the machine. Little wonder therefore, that some beginners get off to a bad start. In the hands of a competent rider motorcycle safety can be virtually assured. Once you have learned enough about motorcycling, it will not be difficult to convince your family and friends that the safety of motorcycle riding is largely a matter of the person who is riding it.

Generally a motorcyclist is young, a newcomer to the streets and highways. He is in the accident-prone category regardless of his vehicle. Inexperience is an abnormal risk at any time, yet again the motorcycle will get the blame. Surely the best way to save lives is to give the beginner experience. The sooner the legal age that boys and girls acquire automotive road sense the better, instead of delaying that experience to the more reckless adolescent age. A yearning in the life of a teenager is to have a "driver's" license and a "putt-putt" of his own. There is reason to encourage this desire. A year's experience on two wheels is about the best assurance that a rider will become a safe and tolerant driver. Experts already agree that the best car drivers are usually those who learned to ride on two wheels. Although accident statistics never indicate whether the driver had any cycling experience, it is probable that those who started as children on bicycles and then rode motorcycles have better driving records than those with no previous experience.

With the exodus from city to suburb, many young wives need an extra vehicle.

Most youngsters today would actually prefer to start with a motorcycle before becoming old enough to have a car. Each time you hear the usual warning "don't let him have a motorcycle," the reason may be because youngsters are unable to get the knowledge of riding and road sense that is part of ownership. Every hobby has some element of risk (such as boxing and football) which is considered normal to development and the acceptance of responsibility. Sportsmen generally are proud of the way they perform. With proper instruction motorcycle riders can learn to tell good from bad riding, and take equal pride in their performance.

The age when a child is first introduced to wheels is much younger now than in the past. The introduction of stabilizer wheels on small cycles allows a child to begin at three an activity that used to start at six. Such early progress may have something to do with the readiness of today's teenager for motorcycling and power driving.

The largest concentration of motorcycles is perhaps at a college campus where each parking area resembles a motorcycle factory yard crowded with new machines. And when young people start work today their first pay check often goes toward a down payment on a motorcycle. This has become a natural and reasonable trend and an ideal way of getting to work, doing errands, and enjoying leisure time outdoors.

Many families have moved from the cities to the suburbs and this has created an additional need for

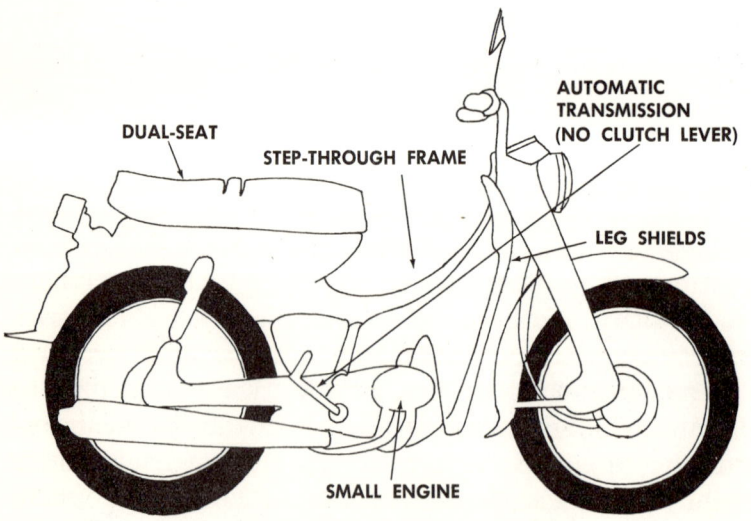

A typical light utility machine.

KING OF THE ROAD

People the world over are quick to appreciate the virtues of today's rugged and economical lightweight machines.

some kind of extra vehicle. Most suburban homes are usually some distance away from the shopping center, train or bus depot. A motorcycle can be a real convenience in a family whose members are always fighting for the car.

In many parts of the world the rising standard of living will undoubtedly result in a great increase in motorcycling—particularly in remote places where there is no public transportation. In young countries where there is not a fully developed industry and where agriculture is not sufficiently mechanized to raise the individual productivity, this mode of transport is only beginning. Crated into aircraft, these little vehicles can be delivered to remote places where even the cost of air freight makes ownership a worthwhile proposition.

Replacing the rickshaw and the donkey comes the motorcycle with power that appeals to workers everywhere.

Already a start has been made to replace the traditional four-legged power supply by a motorcycle hauling a two-wheeled trailer of the rickshaw type. As the output of each man and woman rises, the investment in a motorcycle will help to increase that output even more. Whether far or near, it will also provide more opportunity for leisure. Many of these countries seeking a voice in world affairs are now manufacturing their own motorcycles and scooters. It is here also where the beginner will take to riding. Scarcity of cheap cars and low wage scales bring the lightweight motorcycle into great demand. The smallest and most economical motor vehicle on the road anywhere in the world is surely the motorcycle.

It is also a wonderful experience to go by motorcycle into another country and meet people in their part of the world. A ride along any of the up-to-date streets in the oppressive heat of the tropics is a most invigorating experience. The climate in these places is favorable to year-round riding and the use of a motorcycle can be even more widespread than in Europe, Canada or North America.

4. COME—VISIT WITH ME

When I was a child in London, I used to watch the grown-up girls crowd out of the factories and rush off to the movies or the dance hall. I quaked at the sight and it made me feel very depressed. "That's not going to be the life for me," I said to myself. I also implied it to my parents. They thought I was a bit odd and said it was out of the question for a girl to have silly ideas about adventure. To them, the only way to live respectably was to stay at home, find myself a husband, and settle down to a life of cooking and needlework.

All my life I have known I could never stay cramped in a nine-to-five job with a bus ride and an evening at a show for my share of fun. So I told my friends that I was going to travel—to see Africa and the Sahara Desert, Hollywood, the Grand Canyon, New York and Paris. Then maybe, write a book.

I started to do something about it by sneaking out my brother's bicycle and teaching myself to ride. Later, I found myself staring wide-eyed at motorcycles instead of boys. I admit I had to fight a bit at home to get my way. My parents soon found out that I was actually riding a *motorcycle*. When I was seventeen, they told me that unless I settled down I would end up being nobody's bride. We had an argument about it, with the result that I left home in tears—to find my girl-friend upset about something else. Some of her family had moved to Capetown, South Africa, and she missed them very much.

"Cheer up," I suggested thoughtfully. "Suppose we use my motorcycle and go to see them?" This was the beginning of my first adventure. From then on, my

KING OF THE ROAD 29

Already a start has been made to replace the traditional four-legged power supply by a motorcycle hauling a two-wheeled trailer of the rickshaw type. As the output of each man and woman rises, the investment in a motorcycle will help to increase that output even more. Whether far or near, it will also provide more opportunity for leisure. Many of these countries seeking a voice in world affairs are now manufacturing their own motorcycles and scooters. It is here also where the beginner will take to riding. Scarcity of cheap cars and low wage scales bring the lightweight motorcycle into great demand. The smallest and most economical motor vehicle on the road anywhere in the world is surely the motorcycle.

It is also a wonderful experience to go by motorcycle into another country and meet people in their part of the world. A ride along any of the up-to-date streets in the oppressive heat of the tropics is a most invigorating experience. The climate in these places is favorable to year-round riding and the use of a motorcycle can be even more widespread than in Europe, Canada or North America.

4. COME—VISIT WITH ME

When I was a child in London, I used to watch the grown-up girls crowd out of the factories and rush off to the movies or the dance hall. I quaked at the sight and it made me feel very depressed. "That's not going to be the life for me," I said to myself. I also implied it to my parents. They thought I was a bit odd and said it was out of the question for a girl to have silly ideas about adventure. To them, the only way to live respectably was to stay at home, find myself a husband, and settle down to a life of cooking and needlework.

All my life I have known I could never stay cramped in a nine-to-five job with a bus ride and an evening at a show for my share of fun. So I told my friends that I was going to travel—to see Africa and the Sahara Desert, Hollywood, the Grand Canyon, New York and Paris. Then maybe, write a book.

I started to do something about it by sneaking out my brother's bicycle and teaching myself to ride. Later, I found myself staring wide-eyed at motorcycles instead of boys. I admit I had to fight a bit at home to get my way. My parents soon found out that I was actually riding a *motorcycle*. When I was seventeen, they told me that unless I settled down I would end up being nobody's bride. We had an argument about it, with the result that I left home in tears—to find my girl-friend upset about something else. Some of her family had moved to Capetown, South Africa, and she missed them very much.

"Cheer up," I suggested thoughtfully. "Suppose we use my motorcycle and go to see them?" This was the beginning of my first adventure. From then on, my address was just as likely to be General Delivery, desert edge gas pump, Algiers or Albuquerque.

During the previous years, I had been studying engineering at the University of London. I was an active member of a motorcycle club and had competed in all branches of the sport, such as trials, scrambles and road-track racing. This gave me experience in maintenance and I felt confident that I could take care of a machine under almost any circumstances.

About a thousand Londoners saw us off to cross Africa. We were to say "How d'ye do" to natives who had never seen a motorcycle before. As a discouragement to lions, we took a powerful flashlight and any unfriendly tribesman found himself looking at two businesslike revolvers. For almost a whole year, come-what-may, we were to be our own counselors.

We endured some exasperating experiences such as wearing out a crankshaft in the desert, running out of fuel in the jungle, and eating the remainder of bread so hard that we had to split it with a hammer and screwdriver. The unpleasantness of these experiences was forgotten, however, at the sights and splendor of darkest Africa and our goal which was Table Mountain, 3,550 feet high, before Capetown.

Although I missed my home and family very much, nothing could deter me from seeing more of the world. Unfortunately these ambitious intentions, as well as those of most other people, took a set-back at the outbreak of World War II.

My seven years of active service during the war years followed. I joined a transport corps as soon as the Women's Auxiliary Territorial Service was mobilized.

Thousands of miles of convoy work in air raids and blackouts necessitated special means of communication and transport. I was issued a motorcycle and became the first woman dispatch rider in the British Army. Soon motorcycle riding members of the A.T.S. were competing against regular army, navy, home-guard, and civil defence units in various cycle events.

Toward the end of the war the transport corps was absorbed into base workshops. Two years before demobilization I was transferred to a unit of the Royal Electrical & Mechanical Engineers. I was disappointed that women did not rally to the workshops quicker. Again I pioneered and became the first woman to pass the mechanics fitter's test. For this, the Colonel who was an electrical engineer in civilian life, made me the Women's Auxiliary "trial horse." I was very lucky to have the opportunity of going through the various workshops, which included tank testing and dynamometer engine testing experience. I worked with each foreman for several months, going through every phase of army machine shop activity. Many men did not get the opportunity that I had. The purpose was to decide to what extent certain work could eventually be taken over by women. "And who," I remember saying, "could be more suited for the sensitive touch necessary for Diesel nozzle hand-lapping?"

The return to "civvy street" had no more cheerful compensation than a white ration book and controlled labor. The curtain of austerity was rising very slowly—perhaps a little too slowly for me. In less than a year I was on the move again. I wanted to see America.

Landing in New York with a motorcycle, I wasn't too concerned about reservations, finances, luggage, or any of the other grievous encumbrances essential to most travelers. Equipped with a sleeping bag and a pair of saddle bags which devoted more space to maps and wrenches than to nylons and clothes, I managed to trek along very well.

In 2½ years I had worked at 18 jobs. I had covered 32,000 miles and I had seen America. When I finally got back to London I was able to answer the question, "What is it like over there?"

My heart was still in motorcycling when I returned to the States. Unable to get a suitable opportunity in the trade I started a motorcycle shop of my own: The Motorcycle Riding School of Instruction (later to become Easy Motorcycle Riding Schools Inc.) became an important part of this venture. I have derived great pleasure from the success of graduate motorcyclists and appreciate how much I have learned from them.

5. A BETTER UNDERSTANDING

Each year manufacturers invest more money and improve their equipment to make better motorcycles. With today's beautiful, comfortable, and reliable machines, you have only to get astride one to realize that there is more to those machines than meets the eye. Perhaps it is their technical advancements together with such good design that has made cycles so attractive. Routine maintenance, as well as overhauls and repairs, have become much less frequent. It is now possible to own a machine without continually fiddling with it.

Teledraulic front-fork steering and the swinging-arm rear suspension with telescopic dampers make today's motorcycles very stable and safe even over the

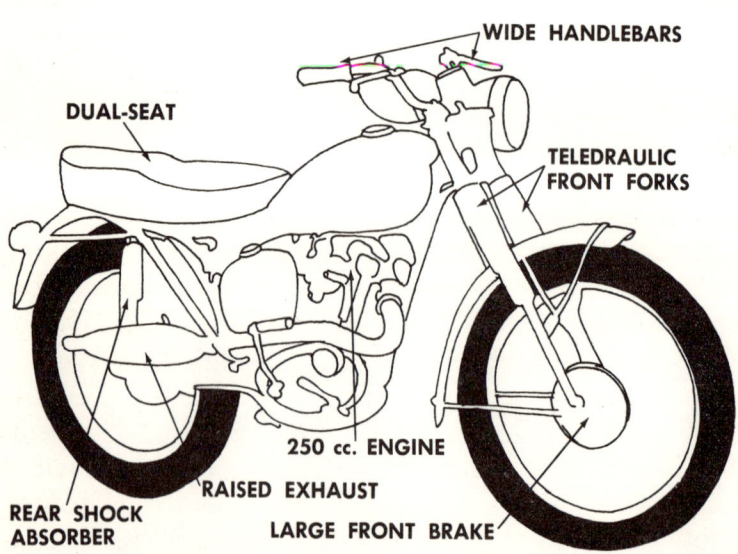

Typical light motorcycle, for touring and off-highway riding.

A BETTER UNDERSTANDING

roughest ground. Good steering enables them to negotiate curves and sharp corners with normal handling and without anxious moments. Sometimes with button starting and weather protection (fairing), synthetic and practically non-skid tires, the motorcycle as a vehicle is able to take its rightful place in the overall transportation picture. They are invaluable for commuters. Today's traffic tangles have turned many a car driver to the more agile two wheeler. Altogether, with good lighting equipment for night riding and powered by a smooth, easy-starting engine fitted with a quiet muffler, it is reasonable enough for almost anyone to be interested. However, the manufacturer can go only so far.

One of the best ways to become a good rider is for you to understand your motorcycle better. As you examine it closely in a way that perhaps you never thought of doing before, there are several important things you will notice. Use a little imagination and take your mind back to the designer's drawing board. Try to visualize the issue and how each one of those points affects your riding.

Every vehicle, whether it is a ship, a plane, a wheeled overland means of conveyance, even a spaceship, is governed by the same laws of physics. A motorcycle is no exception. Each type of vehicle, whether it is to be used to travel in water, in the air, on land, or in outer space, has its own distinctive method of making use of its medium. The type of vehicle governs the way it must be designed, and the ways the laws of motion, gravity, and certifugal force will be applied.

The designer of any type of vehicle has one important point to consider before he can submit any plans to the manufacturer. The question is "What will it have to carry?" The answer—the payload. Of course, those who manufacture vehicles will have other considerations, such as safety and profit, but these will ultimately depend on the kind of payload to be carried.

The load, as well as the vehicle, is subjected to the laws of physics.

Weight is an important factor because of its effect on the control of the vehicle. An example of this is a ship at sea. Sailors learned that after a vessel delivered its cargo (payload), it could not make the return journey without taking on another load. If it happened that there was no replacement payload, then the ship would have to take aboard a dead load, or ballast. Sailors found that in bad weather, an unladen vessel was too light to control.

Furthermore, the mere presence or absence of load is not the only important factor. The way in which the load is handled must also be considered. Returning to our analogy, loose cargo proved no problem to sailors in smooth waters, but shipwrecks occurred when unrestrained masses shifted in heavy weather. Most likely, if the proper load had been accurately positioned and securely fastened before the journey, the ship would have survived the perilous conditions it encountered.

For a ship, proper positioning and control of weight means that the heaviest loads should be in the center of the ship and lower than the horizontal water line, secured low in the hull. Very little of the weight should be stored high or loaded on deck. Load is an influential and effective "control." On a motorcycle, the rider is the load. The machine is quite responsive to shifts in the weight of the rider, and is in fact, partially controlled in this way.

On the designer's drawing board you will notice a horizontal center line or axis passing through each wheel spindle. It is an imaginary line or reference mark related to the center of gravity (c.g.) of the machine. The c.g. is the point about which weight is evenly balanced. The center of gravity is intended to be a little below this horizontal line and as close to the ground as is reasonable. The lower it is, the more stable the machine. It will not feel top-heavy and therefore

A BETTER UNDERSTANDING 37

will be easier to ride and less likely to get out of control. The stability of an unladen machine (except for the fuel in the tank) is at a fixed and safe point. The designer of almost every type of vehicle except a motorcycle plans for a fixed load. Most vehicles are provided with a built-in means of control. A car, for example, has differential gears to take care of centrifugal force as it rounds curves and a four-wheel suspension to equalize shifting passenger loads and irregularities in the road surface.

The motorcycle, among all vehicles, is an oddity. It is a vehicle with a constantly movable or adjustable load—the rider. The rider actually has the ability to transcend the mechanical controls. There are no adapters or levers to manipulate by hand or foot that can give the same result that a skilled rider will obtain by the correct movement of his own weight.

There is no mystery about the fundamentals of good riding. When you sit on your machine you change the center of gravity by the addition of your own weight. You have raised it to the extent of the dual-seat height above that horizontal line. Whether you stand up or sit down makes no difference to your actual weight except that you have raised or lowered it, thus moving your own center of gravity. The center of gravity of the machine has been designed to lie centrally between the wheels, for good stability. As the rider moves forward on the seat, his center of gravity approaches a location directly above the center of gravity of the machine. This brings more weight toward a central location, thus improving the stability. So the weight of the rider and the weight of the machine act more as a single unit, giving a steadier ride. Most of the time it is not necessary to obtain additional control by standing up on the footrests.

This brings us to the subject of "fixed" controls—those means by which you control your motorcycle without using functional or movable controls such as

A BETTER UNDERSTANDING

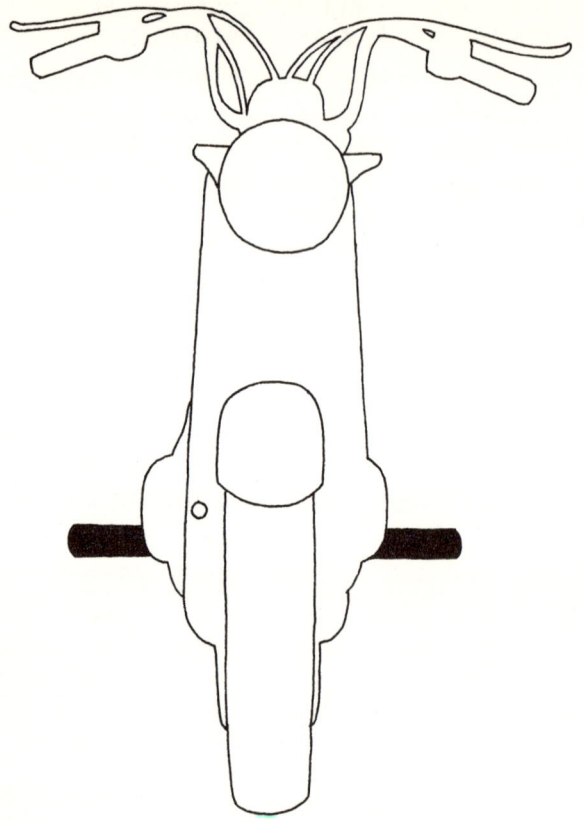

Your footrests are regarded as fixed controls.

the brake or handlebar. Your footrests are regarded as "fixed" controls. The manufacturer of your motorcycle intended it to be stable, but the rider has to keep it so. When you are as experienced as you were with your bicycle you will be able to prove the accuracy with which you can steer by your footrests. When your footrests are equally loaded, the machine will be practically self-steering straight ahead at all except the slowest speeds.

This is only part of what your footrests can do. Your single-track vehicle is designed to steer in the

A BETTER UNDERSTANDING

direction in which it is leaning and much of the imbalance due to cornering can be compensated for by foot pressure or weight applied to the "outside" footrest. As you learn to turn corners, test this for yourself when you are practicing. While going along very slowly in a straight-line path and standing upright on the footrests, slip the clutch and reduce speed to a crawl and you will detect that the steering will turn in the direction of the footrest bearing more of your weight. If your footrest loading is alternately left then right, then steering will go from side to side the same way.

If you put greater weight on your left foot, your machine will turn in that direction.

Your footrests are good stabilizers. Footrests should be level and strong enough to bear your full weight. They should be mounted in a position lower than the unladen (without rider) c.g. for ordinary riding. Contrary to the impression given by bad riders, the motorcycle is a vehicle with a high degree of safety and stability. The distinction between the beginner and the expert rider is perhaps the extent to which all controls —movable and fixed, are used effectively.

Physics tells us that loading (weight) and friction (traction) are related—the greater the weight, the greater the friction. All too often as a beginner gets astride his machine, there is a notion that these physical laws of nature no longer apply.

The traction point is quite a small area considering the force you impose on it when you open the twistgrip and increase your speed. It is therefore of the utmost importance that there always be enough weight on your traction point. Keep your feet up on the footrests thus applying your own weight low on the machine when needed. Never put a foot down to the ground at any time when moving. A foot along the ground will decrease friction by taking some of your weight off the traction point. Further, the manufacturer has provided your machine with efficient shock absorbers to prevent wheel-bounce and absorb irregularities in the ground over which you ride. But much of their effectiveness will depend upon their being loaded by your weight.

When you travel faster, the length of time the traction spot of your rear wheel spends in contact with the ground decreases according to your increase in speed. This requires you to alter the loading of the machine as your speed increases.

With the introduction of the dual-seat instead of the old-fashioned saddle and fixed position you can augment that loading by sliding back on the seat. Then your own weight will be more directly above the

A BETTER UNDERSTANDING 41

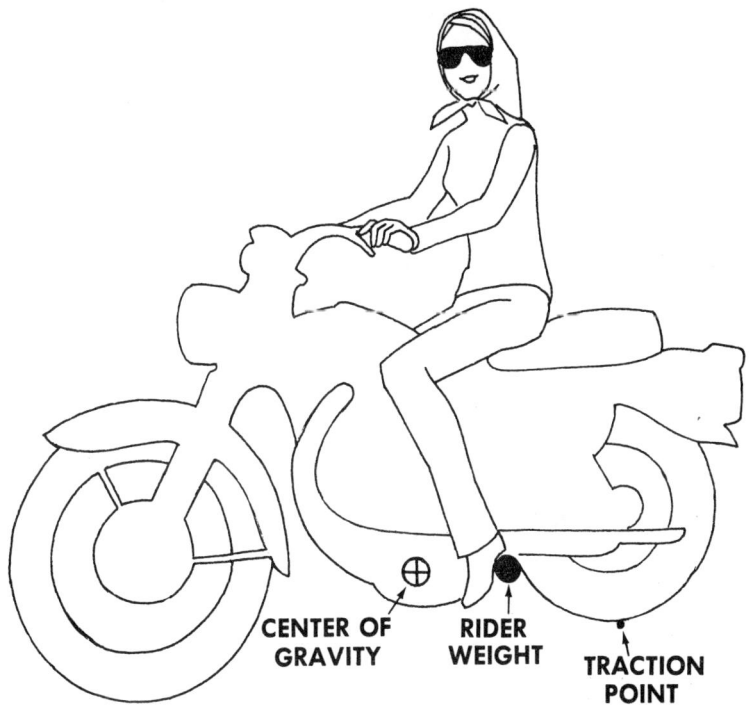

Ride forward on your seat so that your weight is applied closest to the center of gravity of the machine.

traction point, thus giving your rear wheel the maximum adhesion to the road. The further you are away from the handlebars, the more you will lean forward to reach them. Straight arms at high speed help to dampen out any tendency for the steering to speed-wobble and you will be in a suitable attitude to decrease your wind resistance considerably. You have also moved your own center of gravity farther back. Although it is no longer directly above the center of gravity of the machine, this position can be satisfactory as long as you continue to travel in a fairly constant direction.

Although sometimes your machine responds better with your weight (c.g.) close to the c.g. of the machine, there are times when results are better with your weight farther back over the traction point. Your first few miles of traveling at high speed, or, in fact, when riding fast at any time, should not be simply daring, but instead you must ride with clear understanding and effectiveness. It is the combination of overconfidence and bad riding that gives the false impression that motorcycles are dangerous.

Some people believe that anyone who knows how to ride a bicycle and drive a car can get astride a motorcycle and ride it. To a certain extent this is true, but statistics show that the majority of motorcycle accidents occur in the first few hundred miles or within the first year of ownership. With regard to technique there is no comparison between riding a bike and driving a car. A car does not have a clutch and accelerator or rear-view mirror mounted on the movable steering wheel as we have these controls on the handlebars. We do not have a seat to take the weight off our feet, but instead a saddle poise.

The cornering of cars and motorcycles is com-

At high speed, shift your c.g. back above the traction point to give your rear wheel maximum road adhesion.

A BETTER UNDERSTANDING 43

pletely different: you "drive" a car, and you "ride" a motorcycle, using your weight to corner the vehicle other than by use of the controls. The importance of this effect when riding should be understood and the beginner made aware of his weight distribution and the purpose of certain riding positions. Even the most experienced riders will admit that bad habits creep in. Good riders are attentive and will notice these things and correct them. The two significant areas that you will become very much aware of as you gain experience and learn to handle your motorcycle skillfully are the center of gravity and the rear-wheel (driving) traction point. These are the underlying things that contribute a great deal to the understanding of motorcycle riding.

Throughout your daily life you encounter the laws of physics. How safely you ride will depend on how carefully you observe them. We have touched upon the center of gravity and the relationship between weight and traction. We now take into account our movement from one place to another that is affected by the law of inertia. Like any other mass, you will continue to move at the same speed and in the same direction until acted on by an outside force. Whether that outside force is your twistgrip to increase your speed or your brakes to slow down, each of these two forces has to overcome your inertia—the tendency to resist change of motion. Your inertia must always be well under control. If it is overcome too late you will not stop in time. If it is changed too abruptly you will lose traction. When the resistance to slowing down is greater than the friction between your tires and the ground, you will skid.

When you are riding, you and your bike possess kinetic energy—the energy of motion. If the bike suddenly stopped (lost its kinetic energy), the law of inertia dictates that you would keep your kinetic energy and go sailing over the handlebars. Doubling

44 A BETTER UNDERSTANDING

Your kinetic energy would send you flying over the handlebars if you made a sudden stop.

your speed gives you four times as much energy and causes you to be thrown that much more violently in the event of a sudden stop. Your brakes are made to use up this kind of power by applying friction to the turning wheels. The heat generated is easily used up and quickly dissipated. An over-adjusted front brake can impair your riding. The front shock absorber (front forks) is sensitive to a very light application of your front brake hand lever as you slow down and the center of gravity comes forward. The front brake is for this reason at least 25 per cent more powerful than the rear one.

    The force of motion tends to go in a straight line. To stay on a road which is itself changing direction, you and your motorcycle have to overcome the tendency to continue in that straight line. The sharper the curve, the more "changes of direction" you must make before you have ridden out the curve and the natural straight-line path is again the unchanging direction. This outward thrust is centrifugal force. The safety limit is reached when your outward thrust is more than the traction between your tires and the

A BETTER UNDERSTANDING 45

ground. Cornering on two wheels (single track) is quite safe even at high speed, but only provided your tires can be assured traction.

Tire pressure is something you should bear in mind as it affects your traction point. Pressure changes with the temperature. On a cold morning your tires will

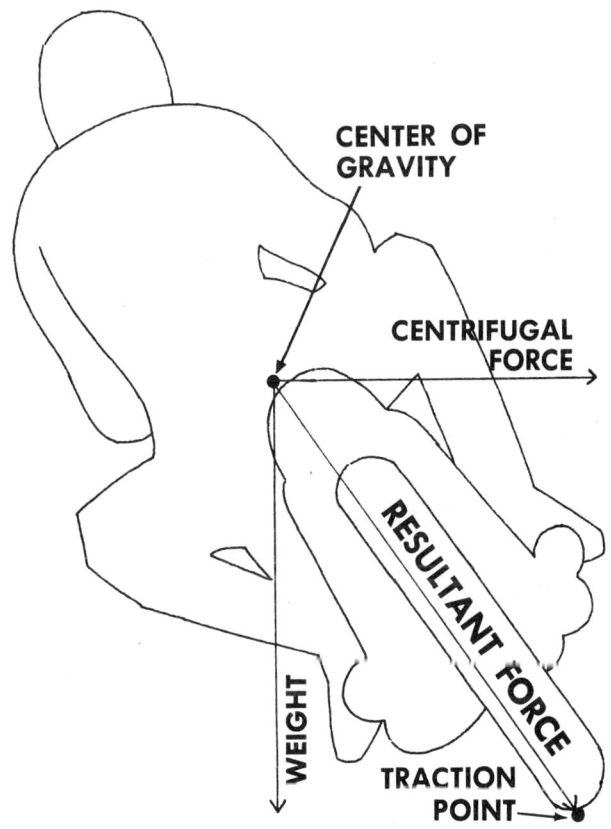

A motorcycle is cornered primarily by leaning, not steering. By leaning into the turn at the proper angle, the *outward* centrifugal force (caused by the change of direction) and the *downward* force of weight combine to form a resultant force that acts at the traction point.

be a little softer. Tire pressures are very important to a motorcyclist.

When you are learning, all corners should be taken carefully with both feet firmly on the footrests. You never know when a slippery spot is going to crop up and you should be able to handle an awkward situation that would be disaster to a less knowledgable rider. Experience will teach you to be aware of the effect of yourself upon your bike apart from the use of the mechanical controls.

For a long time manufacturers have been very much concerned with such issues as where and how to mount the engine which affects the c.g. and consequently the stability. The placing of controls and the position of the seat in the old days used to be in peculiar places. Throughout the years many steps have been taken toward efficiency and better handling—and better roads. Some of the early machines were no more than converted bicycles. Those antique machines with plenty of controls to fiddle with were the forefathers of today's powerful and efficient machines. It was not easy to convince anyone in those days that such out-of-the-ordinary things would ever be of any use. Mechanical troubles were plentiful, the machines were

This steam-powered motorcycle was built by Pierre and Ernest Michaux in 1869.

The difference between the beginner and the expert is the extent to which all controls—fixed and movable—are effectively used.

unreliable and there was more wayside tinkering than riding.

The time has now gone when the motorcycle was considered noisy and dirty, of interest to the mechanically inclined youth, and ridden only by daredevils. Today's beautiful products of engineering are a far cry from the rigid bone-shaking bicycle-with-engine of yesterday. The pneumatic tire, alone, was an innovation of tremendous importance to motorcycles as it has been to all wheeled transport.

Progress was obtained by the same means as that which helped to develop both the bicycle and the automobile: racing. Racing and testing motorcycles by individual as well as factory riders has produced a wide range of roadster models. Every motorcycle today has inherited some feature or other derived from the benefits of competition. Engine performance and handling qualities of standard catalogue models are not always much different these days from their racing prototypes.

When you invest in a machine of your own, you will want to be good enough to get the best out of it. Good riding has a lot to do with machine performance. If you are pleased with the machine you have bought, then you should not allow yourself to have unsafe habits and bad riding faults. Many motorcycle riders have not been instructed in the logic and know-how of two-wheel riding. The one thing you do not purchase when you buy your motorcycle is the ability to ride it. You must want to be good and you will find that enthusiasm and skill usually go together. Motorcycle design will continue to change, but never the basic principles of good riding.

6. GETTING ACQUAINTED

Let us assume that you are one of the beginners for whom this book has been written. If you have not yet obtained your own machine or been able to get hold of something suitable to learn on, then you should put your trust in the name of a reputable manufacturer and choose one. Obtain a catalogue of the various models listed and study the specifications to help you decide. You may depend on information from manufacturers' advertisements and pamphlets.

A new machine will give you warranty protection. If you have in mind a used machine, especially if it is an imported make, be sure that there is factory authorized service in your area. Most machines are reviewed in the trade press and it is possible that you may have read a road test report that was interesting. Sometimes a few good machines are brought into the country as personal baggage by a traveler from abroad. These machines may be intriguing, but if there is no dealer anywhere near you, there will be no service or spare parts when needed.

When you have finally taken the big step of getting your first machine, be sure to learn to handle the machine correctly from the start. Give yourself time to practice and above all think carefully of exactly what you are doing before you handle the controls. Allow yourself sessions in a parking area or on private ground before actually going for a ride on a public street. Above all, do not take a strange machine out of the restricted place where you practice knowing only how to get started and how to stop. Unfortunately, there is the tendency for most beginners to want to

GETTING ACQUAINTED

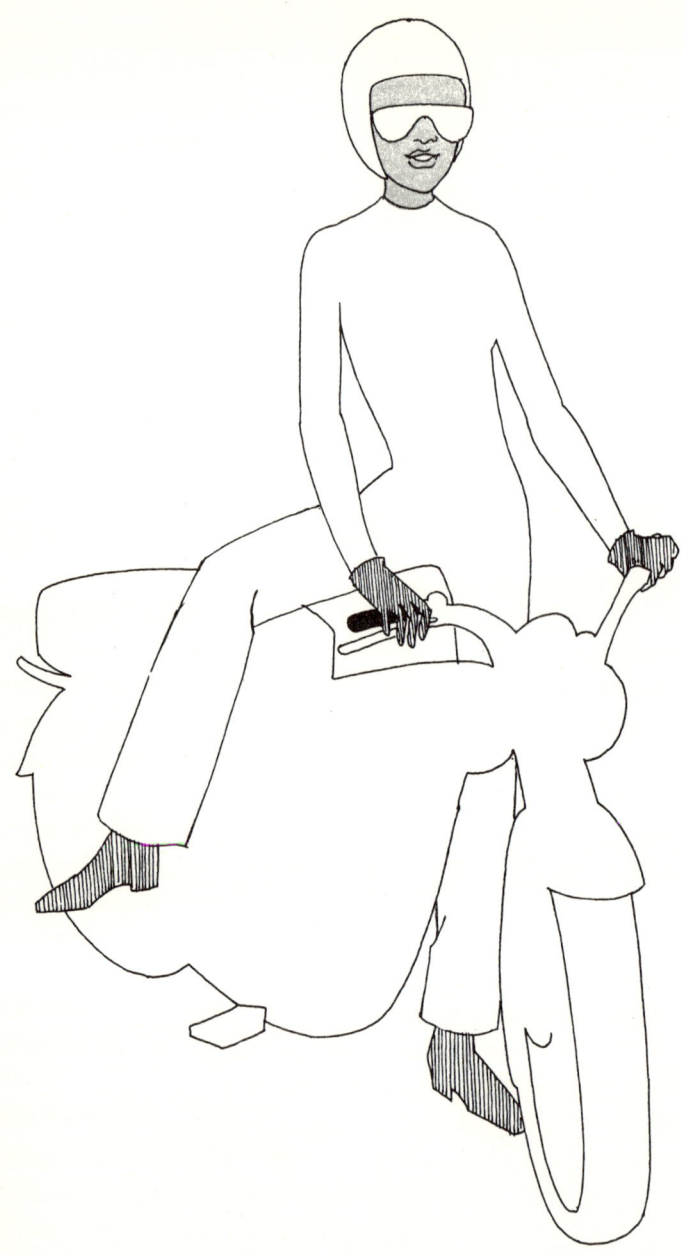

Before mounting, always engage the front brake to prevent the machine from rolling forward as you get astride.

GETTING ACQUAINTED 51

ride before they know enough or have fully mastered each phase. The machine should never be permitted to get into any awkward position that you cannot correct. Practice from information learned by reading and from other riders and prepare for the situations that you will undoubtedly encounter later. Presumably, of course, you know how to ride a bicycle.

As soon as you touch your motorcycle you show what kind of rider you are or, hopefully, going to be. The way you mount is quite important. If you do not have good control at this early stage, there will be little wonder about what happens if you get confused while riding.

It is usual to mount from the left side. For the right-handed majority, this position gives basic natural balance. As you push the machine off the center-stand, be sure your right hand is in control of the front brake so you can stop it from rolling away when the wheels touch the ground and while you get astride. You will feel awkward standing on one foot while the machine starts rolling away before you get on it. One leg is not the best way to support yourself under any circumstances, much less hold up a motorcycle. The footrest on that side will then bang it and you will look really clumsy. Hold the machine steady by applying the front brake. If the engine is running, be sure you can use the hand brake without turning the twistgrip and increasing the engine revolutions. The right-hand rubber handlebar grip (twistgrip) is a built-in accelerator. Rolling or twisting the rubber grip relative to the handlebar regulates the opening and closing of the throttle and the amount of fuel supplied to the engine. Brace yourself against the machine held firmly braked and you will get astride with ease and confidence no matter how big or heavy it may at first appear to be.

At the start everything will seem strange because you are not familiar with the controls and where they are positioned. It can—and does—easily happen that

GETTING ACQUAINTED

a beginner will unintentionally knock the gear lever into gear with a wandering foot while mounting and groping for the footrest. Obviously if it should go in to gear, it will run away with you. As you snatch at the handlebar and accidently open the twistgrip, it will get away faster. You need not worry about anything like that happening if you follow thoughtful procedure. Place your left foot firmly on the ground as you get astride such that you can depend on it to support you and where it will be out of the way of the gear lever. Put your brake foot up on the footrest. Position yourself so you now hold the machine by the rear-wheel brake with your hands free. Every machine has two separate and independent brakes. Hand brake for the front wheel and foot brake for the rear wheel.

The location of foot controls is now standard on all machines. Your right foot should always hold the brake, left foot on the gear pedal. Always take up the correct position as soon as you get astride and put yourself in complete command of the proper control. Brake foot up on its footrest in control of the rear brake; gear foot on the ground for support. Hands free.

Exercises practiced while you are learning will very

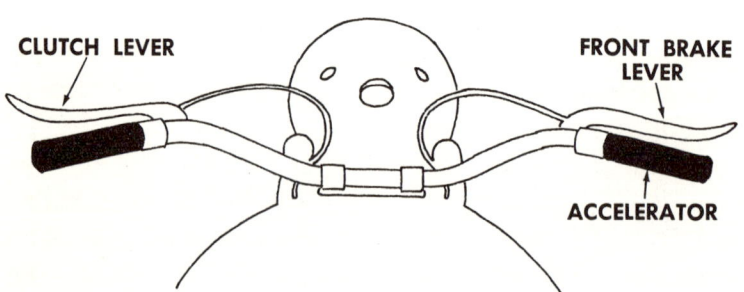

Handlebar controls are in the same position on all machines.

GETTING ACQUAINTED

As soon as you get astride, put your brake foot up, keep your gear foot down and your hands free.

likely be outgrown as you gain experience. However, to sit correctly on your machine while it is stationary is one of the important points and the kind of habit that should be developed.

The position of handlebar controls is the same on all machines. Motorcycle controls are much more directly-connected and have less linkage—and a faster action—than almost any other power-driven vehicle. Your own reaction time is about one sixteenth of a second, and if you are not alert, you may be taken by surprise before realizing what has happened. It is too late then. This short linkage may also explain the apparent sensitivity of the controls. Levers should feel silky smooth and be in a natural position for hands and fingers and an easy movement for each foot. The handlebar is considered a control. It controls the steering. On it are placed controls, so it is like a movable keyboard. With a single-track vehicle such as a motorcycle, steering and stability are affiliated. Arms should be quite flexible to permit freedom of steering.

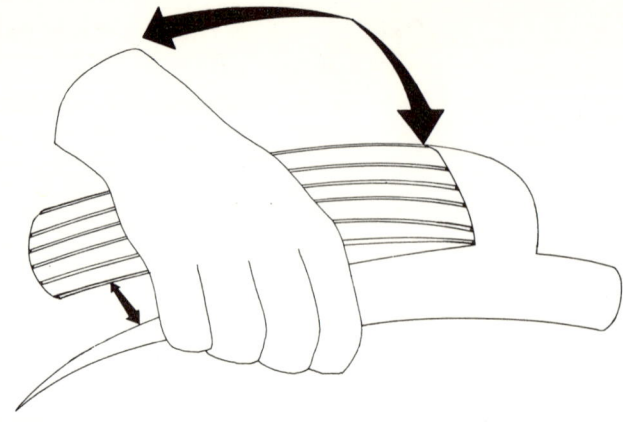

Practice until you can move the right-hand controls in, out and around with ease.

It takes a light arm and good twistgrip hand to keep the engine running smoothly and steer at slow speeds quite sharply to one side or the other so the twistgrip is not in any way affected by handlebar movement. Practice on the center-stand before going a step further until you can move your controls three ways simultaneously and independently, namely: front brake (in/out); steering (left/right); and twistgrip (rotary).

If there is another lever on the right side of the handlebar, it is the air choke used only for starting a cold engine. On many machines the choke is located directly on the carburetor.

The left handlebar rubber grip is rigid. This fixed grip gives you a firm hold to operate the clutch. If there is another lever on the clutch side, it will be a decompressor to aid starting a high compression single cylinder engine. The horn button is also on that side close to your left thumb, but nobody should regard that as a control.

Other controls are not directly related to riding. The gas tank is fitted with fuel taps. Marked on each tap are the following positions: off, main tank, and reserve. The carburetor is gravity fed so it is advisable

GETTING ACQUAINTED 55

to turn off the fuel tap(s) when the machine has to stand for a while or overnight.

The kickstarter pedal on the transmission is coupled to the engine. According to manufacture it could be on either side of the machine, so the model determines which foot you use to start the engine. A persuasive swing downward rather than a kick will turn over the engine rapidly enough to actuate ignition when the IGN switch and fuel are turned on. When an electric starter is fitted, simply switch on the fuel and ignition and push the button.

Electrical switches and their position vary from machine to machine. The two main electrical switches are ignition (high tension) and lighting (low tension). Frequently the two systems are wired together into the same switch. Battery ignition usually has a key and it is advisable to remove it from the switch when the machine is left unattended. The headlight dimmer switch and horn are together within easy reach with-

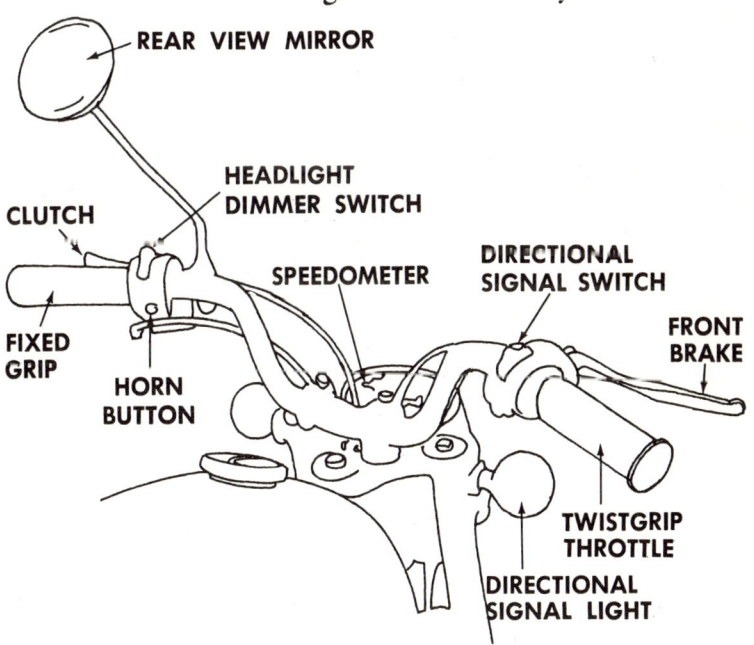

out lifting your hand when riding. The headlight gives high beam, floodlight, or parking light. Some states now require motorcycles to be ridden with their headlights on even during the daylight hours, and some machines even light up automatically when the ignition is turned on. When it comes to visibility, every little bit helps and the comment, "I just didn't see him," is of little value. The rear light operates the brake stoplight and illuminates the vehicle rear number plate.

In most places the law requires a motorcycle to have a speedometer. The odometer reading indicates the total miles traveled while the "trip" indicator can be re-set to zero by hand to record a particular distance. You will find the re-set reading useful to remind you when to refuel.

The tachometer, if your machine has one, indicates engine revolutions. A tachometer can help you to "time" your gear shifts. Good gear shifts are made at the correct engine "speed" whatever your road speed may be.

Out on the open highway, you will be using your steering damper if your machine has one. It is the large knob in the center of the steering column. The faster you travel, the less time the traction spot of your tires spends in contact with the ground with each turn of the wheel and you will feel the steering getting too "light." A turn or so of the steering damper (screw downward) will stiffen the steering and prevent speed-wobble. Use your steering damper wisely and your fast ride will be a safe and pleasant one. Remember to slacken it off as you reduce speed. Stiff steering at slow speeds affects your stability. A tight damper at slow speed produces a weaving effect that will cause you to sway.

Precaution has very likely been taken by the manufacturer of your machine to see that it can not easily be ridden away after you have parked it, by fitting an anti-theft lock in addition to the ignition key. It is installed in the steering head and locks the front forks to one side. Now is a good time to check and see that you have all the necessary keys. You may have three keys altogether apart from spares: ignition, steering lock, and toolbox or pannier compartment.

As you make yourself familiar with your machine, be sure it has been serviced before you ride it. The correct grade(s) of oil should be in the engine, transmission, primary chaincase and front forks. Tire pressures are also important. Normally these preparations will have been carried out already, but check them anyway because you can never be too careful.

Many things will require your attention all at the same time, and since you can not afford divided thinking, a step-by-step method is the most reasonable way to learn to ride. Often the best result comes by doing a job very carefully and taking a little more time. Coordinating the controls must first be accomplished so it may take you a little longer than expected. There is nothing wrong with being a slow learner.

7. THE ART OF CORNERING

A glance at the riders you see turning corners will show that some look better than others. Perhaps it is style that impresses you more than speed. It is hard to describe the differences in cornering except perhaps to say that a skillful rider conforms better to the principles of cornering or change-of-direction. Traffic these days approaches corners and highway curves at speeds that require a high degree of skill by motorcycle riders.

Machines too are subjected to the same demands, but most misfortunes are not due to mechanical faults. A highpower machine is not dangerous in itself. It is quite capable of banking curves placidly without any trouble. One common fear with beginners and also perhaps in the imagination of non-riders is the risk of skidding. The motorcycle should be coming along toward the curve in a straight-line approach as the braking is applied. A straight-line skid at the worst is manageable. It is the thoughtless rider who leaves the braking until it is too late. He will use the brakes in the corner when the machine is leaning over at an angle and the traction point is already holding to the utmost and will soon be in bad trouble without realizing what actually happened. It is not a matter of a motorcycle being unstable, but that the rider heedlessly upset it.

To learn cornering it makes good sense to start slowly and work upward toward faster corners. You will find that meaningful practice is in many ways more interesting than going for a ride, anxious and uneasy, hoping to gain your experience on the streets.

THE ART OF CORNERING

GOOD

Good style for city driving and normal cornering.

Start on the curved part of the turn. Afterward add the straight lines of approach and exit until you have the complete navigation. First, know the turning circle of your machine. Keep your feet up on the footrests and "slip" the clutch if necessary to steer the smallest possible circle consistent with the type of machine you are riding. If you have a very small lightweight to work with it should be possible to make the tiniest turn with the steering as far as it will go (full lock). Feel how turning circles is related to varying speeds. As you go faster, your circles get bigger. To disregard centrifugal force when making a turn is as unreasonable as to think the laws of physics do not exist.

Practice your right (brake side) and left (gear

side) turns. You will find how helpful the brake side footrest can be when you learn to keep your foot on it. Now use half of the complete turn (semicircle) for further practice in first (bottom) gear. Add to that curve the straight line that you intend to use for your approach. No matter how fast you come along that line of approach into your corner, remember to brake before you reach it, when the machine is vertical and on a straight course. Enter the curve just as you practiced it as part of a complete circle immediately before. You are not out of the corner until the rear (driving) wheel axis is in line with front wheel steering. Acceleration just then is really effective and will get you away from the curve in a straight-line path effectively and safely.

To a certain extent cornering will depend on how well you brake and how soon you see into and out of the maneuver. The experienced rider uses both front and rear brakes to the best advantage and you too, will soon learn to give braking your careful attention. Brake design has undergone considerable modification to absorb heat evenly without distortion. Twistgrip control and accurate braking involves self control. Normally your knees are against the sides of the tank. Sometimes in a very sharp corner it will help to flap your "inside" knee away from the tank side. It makes room for the handlebars when steered to one side and takes some of the foot pressure (weight) off that side footrest. Out on the highway the only braking that may be necessary is to "brake on the engine" by closing the twistgrip. Again it depends what type of machine you have. The two-stroke type of engine provides negligible braking when the engine is shut down and is therefore harder on the brakes. The knack of cornering on two wheels is to use the least possible power to maintain the best course or "line" steered, rather than to see how much power (and thereby centrifugal force) you can hold regardless

THE ART OF CORNERING

On a very sharp corner, flap your inside knee away from the tank side to make room for the handlebars.

of line. A skillful rider sweeping into a turn within the legal speed limit in the proper gear and on a true line already determined, is a far safer rider than one who totters round with uncertainty much slower. Do not speed into a turn. Accelerate away from it instead and just when both wheels are with you along the "out" line.

It is important for a motorcycle rider to judge speed accurately. Your speed determines your line. You do not have the auxiliary aids like a two-track vehicle with differential wheels and torsion bars to

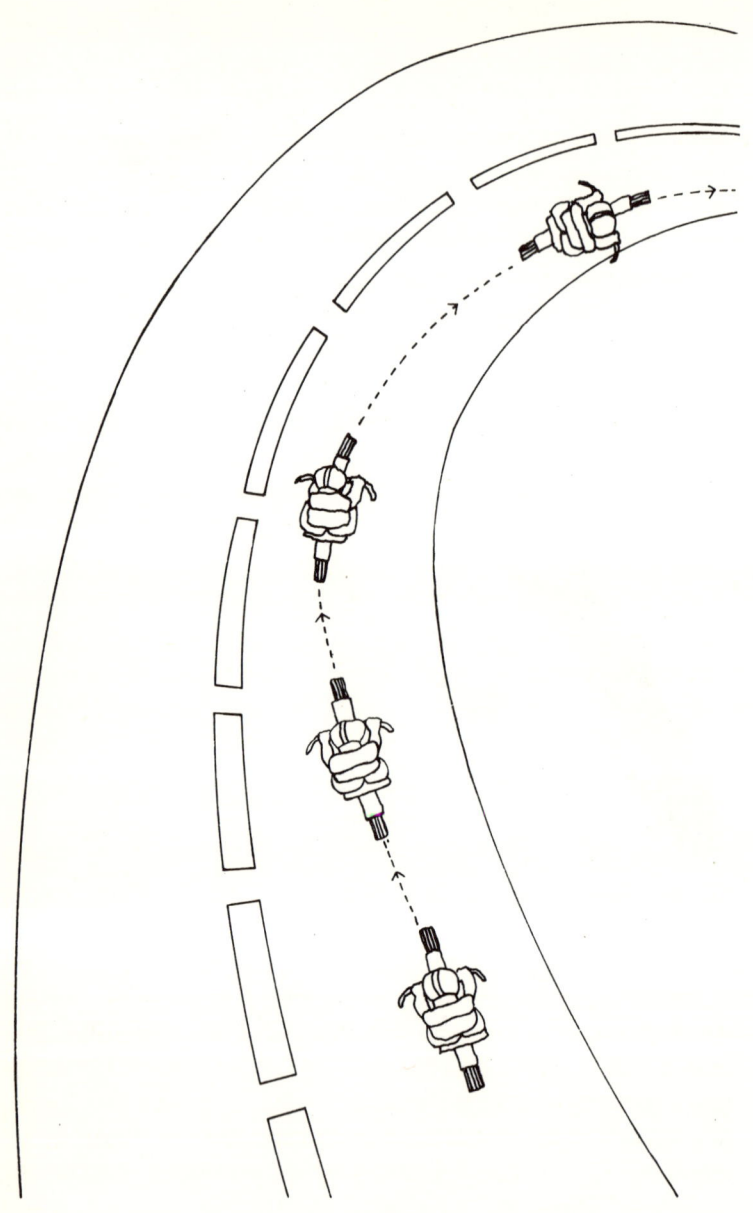

Go in wide and come out close.

THE ART OF CORNERING

On a very sharp corner, flap your inside knee away from the tank side to make room for the handlebars.

of line. A skillful rider sweeping into a turn within the legal speed limit in the proper gear and on a true line already determined, is a far safer rider than one who totters round with uncertainty much slower. Do not speed into a turn. Accelerate away from it instead and just when both wheels are with you along the "out" line.

It is important for a motorcycle rider to judge speed accurately. Your speed determines your line. You do not have the auxiliary aids like a two-track vehicle with differential wheels and torsion bars to

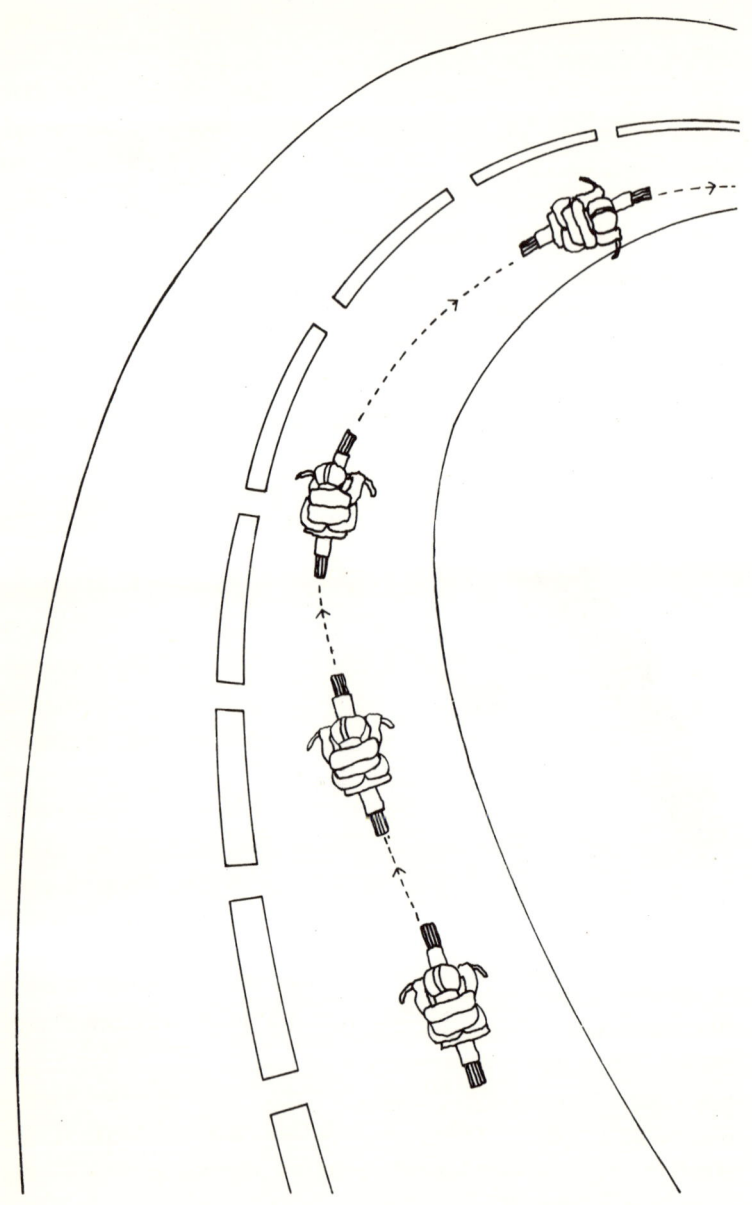

Go in wide and come out close.

THE ART OF CORNERING 63

take up your errors. The shortest path, or radius of the curved section will take the least time. This is the logic behind fast corners. However, that must not induce you to go speeding. It is a simple outline of how to take corners efficiently and to help you to raise your average speed with safety. In racing, the time factor is important, although the characteristics are the same at any corner. As you gain experience at cornering you will associate line with speed. In addition to the mechanical controls you will have good command over your machine free from the manipulation of riding. Unless pupils who are learning can understand "good control" and feel their influence upon the machine under different circumstances, naturally they are not going to be very good riders.

Sharp bends and corners can be ridden in many different ways, but the experts always say, "Go in wide and come out close." Leave plenty of room to drift out in emergency. This might be very useful one day when a curve turns out to be more severe than you anticipated. Every beginner should keep well within the limit of his or her ability until cornering can be capably done. Experience will bring faster corners, but slow speed in first gear is fast enough until you get the feel of it.

Later on, when you approach corners a little faster, be alert for centrifugal force pushing you into an expanding curve. The art of cornering is to blend the three parts of the turn. Determine your line of approach into the turn and adjust your speed as necessary then and there. When you are in the turn, centrifugal force is effective. Put plenty of weight on your traction point by keeping your feet securely up on the footrests. Use them as stabilizers to keep your weight low. Accelerate out as soon as all of you, rear as well as front wheel, is heading out. Generally speaking, you should emerge out of a turn in relation to the line and the speed that you went into it making no midway maneuvers. The lines that an expert rider steers as he lays or leans from one corner to another shows knowledge and the ability to use it.

Never attempt to make up for late time on a trip by riding faster around corners. When you feel that you can follow a good line as you approach your turn and lean into it free from twitching and can then spurt away along the straight without swinging wide, you will have learned how to corner. Develop your own style of riding based on true skill and understanding. When you have demonstrated, if only to yourself, that you can handle your machine then you will be ready to begin exploring the world around you.

8. THE FOOT GEARSHIFT

When you are riding your motorcycle uphill, your engine "speed" or revolutions will drop because of the increased load. Therefore the power will drop also. To maintain the engine revolutions and hence to have enough power to climb hills, a smaller or "lower" gear is required. Similarly for good acceleration from take-off and at higher speeds when more power is required the only way is to change "up" to a higher gear. Your engine performs best only within certain limits of revolution. It is not always realized that except when accelerating or slowing, the power developed depends upon the engine "speed" being within those limits.

Gearshifts are made so that while engine revolutions are within normal limits, the back (driving) wheel turns to suit actual riding conditions and road speed. The manufacturer of your machine has given you the most suitable gear ratio for the size of that engine. Gear ratio information will be in your owner's manual, and referred to, for example, as 20 : 1, which means that the engine makes twenty revolutions to one of the driving wheel in that particular gear. As your gear ratio is reduced—to say 5 : 1—your speed goes up. The bigger gear you have chosen to use will not revolve so many times and has decreased the ratio. If you want your back wheel to go "quicker" so you can go "faster" you shift "up."

Most utility motorcycles have a four-speed transmission. The transmission is designed to transmit power from the engine to the back wheel at whatever road speed you are traveling. Shifting gears will enable you to make every possible demand from your machine without over-exerting the engine.

Already you have learned to co-ordinate the hand controls and foot levers and combine it with balancing and steering. This is quite enough for any beginner without getting involved in gearshifting. All exercises and practice so far have been done in first (bottom) gear. First gear was slow enough (in road speed) to move off and crawl along at walking pace so that you could learn basic control. You are now familiar with your gear foot. You also know how many gears your own particular machine has and the "pattern" or position of the gears. Regardless of which gear you engage, a spring-and-ratchet will return the lever to the original position in relation to your foot on the footrest. A slight steady pressure with your toe is enough to engage the next gear. Vigorous prodding of the gear lever with your foot is quite unnecessary. Either put your toe underneath and lift it up or put your toe on top and push it down. Each time the gear lever is moved when you are riding, whether from one gear to another or a return to neutral, always use the clutch.

Gearshifting should be practiced on a quiet stretch of road where there are no crossings. Do not get panicky and always be careful. Ride along in first gear. Increase road speed (twistgrip) fast enough for second gear and de-clutch (left hand). Move the foot-gearshift lever through neutral, engage second gear, and release clutch all at the same time. Watch where you are going and never look down for the gear lever. At the end of your second-gear run be ready and remember how to make the turn (cornering) to come back. Slow down to first-gear speed. Shifting down to a lower gear also helps to take up some of the force of motion besides brakes to slow your speed in preparation for the turn. When shifting "down," raise the engine

THE FOOT GEARSHIFT 67

"revs" a little. The knack is to bring the high "revs" of the in-coming low gear up to match the fading "revs" of the out-going high gear. Circle around slowly as you have already been doing until your back (driving) wheel is out of the turn and then accelerate away through the gears. Listen or "feel" the engine speed and "time" your gearshifts accurately. Exercise caution not to go too quickly for prevailing road conditions. When you return from your practice run, leave plenty of time to slip out of second gear into neutral before you come coasting in. Your brake foot will be ready to bring you to a halt and your gear foot ready to support you. Hands free.

As you progress with your riding use the gears continuously and learn to obtain the best combinations of engine speeds to road speeds. Riding in top gear is not always very fast, but it will be getting you among other vehicles. So practice your gearshifts before getting involved with traffic in the street. Traffic in itself is a problem. Top-gear speed certainly lessens the time you have to determine your traffic situation. Pay special attention to riding position and have each foot automatically ready for braking or gearshifting without any time lag. It is better to allow the engine to "rev" in a lower gear than to "labor" in the higher one. If you hope to be really good at gearshifting, you should be careful from the beginning. It is not only bad for your machine to make mistakes and "grind" gears; it will also take you longer to correct yourself than to get it right the first time.

While seemingly hard to follow, actually gearshifting is simply a matter of timing. Time your gearshifts in such a way that the speed of the engine (revolutions) and the "revs" for the gear you are going to use next occur as nearly as possible at the same relative speed. Let your imagination make up for your inexperience until you can change gear from take-off to top gear and back to neutral without a jolt. Synchronize your movements so that a passenger riding behind you on the dual-seat can not detect the gearshifts and will enjoy your smooth riding.

When you get used to higher speeds and easy gearshifting you will have learned enough to go beyond your no-man's land. The time has come for you to go for your first real ride. Confine your first trips to quiet streets and try to be back before dark. Pay attention to the finer points that will eventually distinguish you as the better rider. Good motorcycling does not come automatically with mounting mileage.

9. ROADCRAFT

At what stage will you begin to feel that you are really riding? So far you have been concerned with learning to stay aboard, to balance and steer and to feel the effect of the controls. Riding begins with all these attributes plus a skillful blend of power and speed. Roadcraft is concerned with conditions around you quite apart from the relationship between you and your machine. It also includes your observance of the highway code. Now that you are qualified to use every part of your motorcycle effectively, you should also be able to ride at well-judged speed over almost any ground surface in any weather with due regard to traffic laws. As a motorcyclist you must observe the same regulations that apply to other motor vehicles. If you do not have a motorcycle of your own, you should have the consent of the legal owner who is responsible before you ride it. The machine you ride must have a vehicle license. Now you are ready to apply for your test and obtain your riding license. When you pass the test, remember it is the minimum qualification required to ride in public. Don't get the impression it means you are fully competent. In places where insurance is compulsory you must contact an insurance company and obtain a motorcycle policy.

The rule of the road in most countries is to keep to the right-hand side except when overtaking. Look around before you move off even though you may have a rear-view mirror to see that no one is about to overtake you.

Go only when you can do so safely and without inconvenience to other motorists. Check to see that your side-stand is up. The center-stand should spring up automatically. Ride lightly for the first few miles to give the engine a chance to warm up. Thick oil does not flow readily through the close clearances of a motorcycle engine even under oil pump pressure. Riding a cold engine hard before it has had time to warm to normal operating temperature is probably the cause of more broken piston rings and worn cylinders than any other factor. This is the critical period of learning to ride, so give yourself plenty of time to cope with situations as you meet them. Ride relaxed with feet (weight) firmly on the footrests. If you come upon a bad patch in the street, carry on, because your motorcycle is designed to withstand rough going if you can

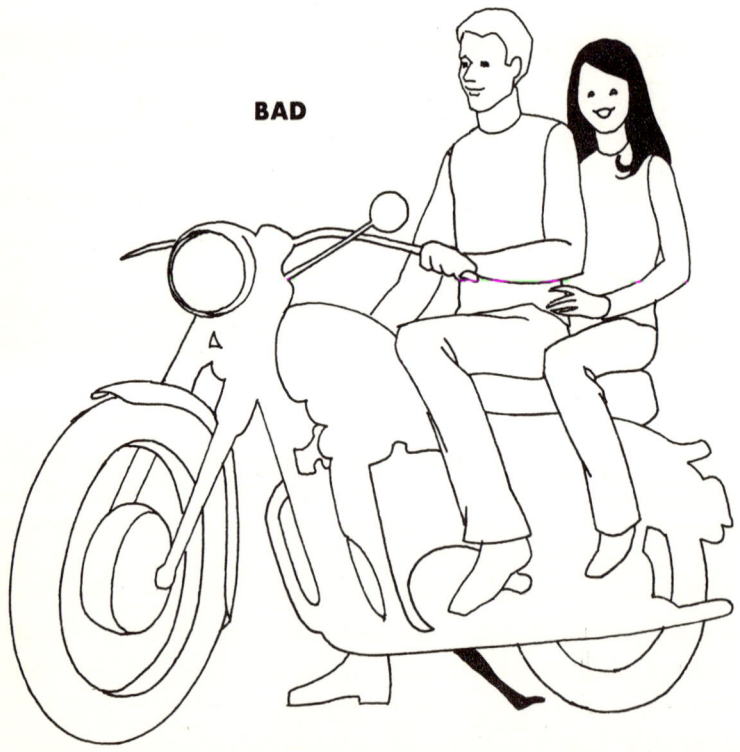

Before starting off, make sure your center-stand has sprung up automatically.

When you hit a bad patch, keep your weight low, rise on your footrests and use your knees as springs.

ride it well enough. Poise on your footrests with weight low and use your knees as additional "shock absorbers" to help your front forks and rear suspension to accept the shock-load as you pass over it.

Remember that you will be on your own. There will not be anybody with you to tell you what to do, but it is very unlikely that you should attempt to suddenly dodge a rough spot. If your machine is in good mechanical condition and you are well and correctly mounted you will learn to depend on your own ability to get you across bad patches.

Now is the time when you should begin to improve your braking. Check your wheels to see if they are the same size or whether the back tire is slightly wider than the front. A slightly wider track at the back will give you a good traction point to work with. However, the less the front and back brakes are used the better. The same power that will accelerate your motorcycle (the engine) is also there to slow you down. Close the twistgrip and reduce engine revolutions to reduce speed. The same can be said about the transmission. Change to a lower gear and let the transmission slow you down. Maintain the high engine "speed" and change back into a higher gear to resume road speed. Engine speed (twistgrip) and gearshifting with a slight touch of both brakes requires good judgement and practice.

To understand better how to apply your brakes, the disposition of the liquid in your tank might help you. Fuel will flow forward as you tend to slow and will sweep to the back of your tank as you accelerate. Your own weight and that of your machine act in exactly the same way. Your front brake is designed to take the heavier load. A good front brake is thus more powerful and less dangerous than a potent back brake. It is far easier to lock the rear wheel with a foot pedal operated control than the front wheel with a hand operated control. In an emergency you would almost certainly apply the brakes as you normally do, but with greater force. Therefore if you are in the habit of using the rear brake only, in an emergency you would almost certainly thrust your foot down, completely forgetting the front brake, and risk the possibility of going into a skid.

Be sure that your brakes are adjusted to give even and gradually increasing pressure on the drums and with the most effective leverage to suit yourself. A common fault is overadjustment, whereas it would be better to lock a wheel later rather then sooner. Never allow your brakes to become jerky due to the linings getting sticky or worn. Since load (weight) and friction (traction point) are proportional you should learn as soon as possible the best way to use your mechanical brakes.

Many riders blame the road surface for skidding and falling off. In fact it was not the road surface that

ROADCRAFT

Brakes should be adjusted to give even and gradually increasing pressure. Don't overadjust them or you may lock a wheel.

caused the trouble, but the way it was ridden. Stay alert, look ahead and you will see any change of road surface. Reduce speed in good time if you feel that it is necessary, but control your machine smoothly over the bad patch with feet up on the foot rests and a very gentle twistgrip hand. Remember that at the opposite end of that throttle control is the traction point with which you are especially concerned. The chief cause of skidding is going too fast in the wrong place. As already explained, a straight-line skid is not difficult to manage, but a side slip due to excessive banking is another matter. Tire pressure has something to do with it. If you do unfortunately skid and can stay upright long enough to remove the cause, it can be controlled. If due to bad braking, release the brake(s) immediately and steer the machine in the direction of the slide, but not any more or another skid will develop in the other direction. Stay astride and keep your feet up and knees in until you regain traction. On wet streets better grip on the road surface can be obtained by slightly reducing the tire pressures.

GOOD

Keep a flexible grip on the handlebars, allow your arms to move freely, and keep your knees along the sides of the tank no matter how your machine takes a big bump.

To a limited extent a motorcycle is affected by wind (aero-dynamic) and by its weight (traction and momentum) and by flywheel influence (gyroscopic) since you cannot remain upright unless you are in motion. Suspension and brake design is sound engineering practice based on these natural laws. Three specific parts of you that are in contact with your machine transfer your weight through the wheels to the ground. These are your feet; seat; knees and thighs, and it is the latter which covers the largest area.

The handlebars are a control, not a grab-rail. Keep your feet on the footrests.

To ride effectively, keep your knees along the sides of the tank. Whether you sit forward or further back will make a difference to your center of gravity and traction point. On loose surfaces or where there are hard bumps or ruts you will discover how to make the best use of your weight by changing your riding position. Learn to control your center of gravity and traction point and then you will have a much better idea about what constitutes good motorcycling.

Steering will be best only if the handlebars are held lightly. Check your steering damper if one is fitted. There should be no unevenness. It should feel smooth from side to side so you can balance easily in slow moving traffic. Steering should be light enough for town riding and stiff (dampened down) enough not to shimmy at high speed. Steering is a control that will aid your stability. It is not a grab-rail. The handlebar has a two-fold job of accommodating the control levers for your hands to operate while at the same time allowing your arms the flexibility to permit the full range of steering. The "bend" of your handlebar should be such that your hands rest naturally on the levers when you are seated normally. You should not have to stick your elbows out in the wind to pull the levers. Unreasonable riding positions and fads by bad riders almost defy common sense. Leaning on the handlebars to imitate a track racer looks bad and will not impress the true enthusiast who knows good riding inside out. Get to know your machine as thoroughly as possible and be careful not to take instruction from some other rider unless you are quite sure he is giving you good advice. He may teach you his own faults without realizing it.

When your machine does not respond as it should, check for mechanical trouble. It is unlikely that anything will break suddenly and if you are attentive enough you can prevent breakdowns.

Your out-in-the-open dual-seat position enables you to see better than other road users. However, it is difficult for others to judge your position and oncoming speed accurately. An approaching motorcyclist gives the impression of speed and it is very difficult to change that illusion. Follow the traffic pattern and keep the same speed. Slowness can be a fault. Even though a motorcycle does not take up much room, a slow rider can easily block traffic and may even be a hazard to himself. Watch the wheels of parked cars and you will have ample warning when someone at the steering wheel is going to pull out.

Hand signals should not present a problem. Approach a road junction in neutral if you anticipate having to yield to traffic or stop. Extend your clutch hand in plenty of time and show a full arm's length signal to indicate your direction. If conditions turn out to be favorable, pop back into gear—either second or first ("up" or "down") according to your speed—and complete the turn. If conditions are not suitable for the turn and you must stop, then your brake foot is ready.

Left turns might be awkward for you in the beginning. Often you have to depend on the courtesy of other road users to let you make the turn, and you will often find yourself exposed in the middle of the intersection until you can get through. One way to avoid this position is to keep to the right and continue to the far corner of the junction or intersection and stop. Wait there. When the cross traffic moves forward you can filter in and go along straight ahead. This bit of advice is in no way illegal. Until you can handle your motorcycle with enough confidence and experience to make difficult maneuvers in traffic in a safe way, this is a simple way to do it.

Bumpers protect car drivers and if you feel that car drivers are not giving you due consideration in dense traffic, then position yourself slightly off-side. This does not mean two-wheeling between lanes. Offside you are less vulnerable and besides there is less oil and grease on the road than in the middle of the lane in case an emergency stop is necessary. Although the driver ahead may not be able to see you in his rear-view mirror because you are riding in his "blind-spot" it is not reasonable or safe for you to expect his consideration. He probably does not understand motorcycles or care about your problem anyway.

Dense traffic does not always travel slowly. Expressways can be worse than race tracks since on the track, the vehicles are well handled. Expressways are faster than the ordinary routes, but there has never been any doubt about them being boring. In the distance the scenic hills and valleys may look beautiful although it does not change the monotony of long stretches of set-throttle riding. If getting to your destination is all that matters and you travel on an expressway then take the lane on the steering-wheel side of cars so the overtaking driver can have a closer view of you. It is also safer to have fast moving traffic only on one side of you so that you have a safety-shoot off the road if you have to escape danger. The faster you figure out the traffic pattern ahead, the more time you have to think about what to do and when to maneuver into your exit lane. Places through which the old route passes have the hills and curves that make a cross country trip on a motorcycle much more fun to ride. Stops in the small towns are certainly more interesting and give a good opportunity to meet the local folk.

You will soon get to know other motorcyclists and you will feel as though you have joined a fraternity. You will examine machines owned by other enthusiasts and perhaps will have an opportunity to ride another "bike." Different machines even though the same model and manufacture perform differently. When you ride a strange machine be careful to feel it out first.

When you refuel at a gas station, be careful how you re-enter the street. Your motorcycle has been handling very consistently without a load of liquid in the tank and you have grown accustomed to this condition. Suddenly you put about thirty pounds of fluid (unstable) weight high above your center of gravity. Make allowance for this change and re-adjust yourself to the difference in handling quality. The same advice can be given when carrying a passenger

ROADCRAFT 79

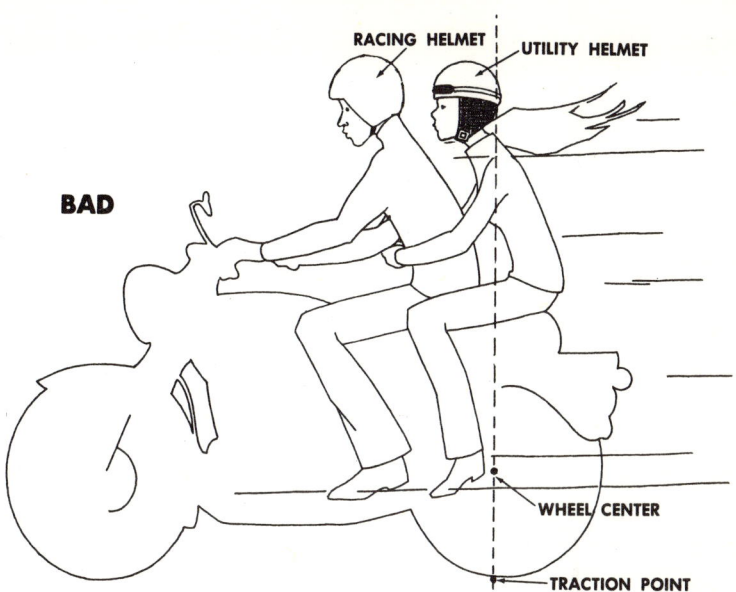

The passenger is sitting too far back to give you maximum control.

behind you on the dual-seat. Weight over which you will have diminishing control is that which is positioned behind a vertical line extended between your traction spot and rear-wheel axle. Sit well forward yourself so your passenger's weight is not beyond this line.

It does not take long to learn how to ride, but it takes a long time to learn how to handle your machine well.

To ride through mud, you need a fast start. Rise on the footrests to lower your weight. Grip the tank with your knees. Once on harder ground, gently start to pick up speed again.

10. ADVANCED RIDING

The ability you have developed following a good training period of street and highway riding will have you well on the way to becoming a veteran. You may now want to try your prowess at advanced riding and take your machine off the road into the countryside. There are special machines for trail riding, but that does not mean your present road model should prevent you from trying it to a limited extent. A standard machine can be modified for off-road riding by changing the tires and the gear ratio and many other things. Actually, a motorcycle should be used only for the purpose for which it was intended and it is not recommended that a trail "bike" be ridden along the street and vice versa. It is understandable, however, that you do not want to invest in special equipment or own two machines until you know what you are getting into. Accomplished indeed is any rider who has reached the limit of his own ability whatever kind of motorcycle he may choose to ride.

Motorcycle exploration into the countryside where you can really get a deep breath of fresh air is particularly enjoyable. The capability of your ordinary machine to climb into the remote places is quite good as you will discover for yourself. Riding over rough ground is really quite safe. You will soon begin to feel with far greater precision the responsiveness of your machine. Soft spots will test and thus improve your riding tremendously after you have acquired the technique. Muddy ground is probably the most difficult kind of surface to ride over. On a slippery surface there is no grip at all. Where there is no grip there can be no torque. To carry you through mud or sand, start fast with impetus enough to get you to the far side while diminishing your engine "revs" correspondingly. Once on harder ground gently start to pick up speed again as you regain traction. In the beginning each "hazard" or rough patch that you are going to negotiate should be pre-inspected. Dismount and survey the area. The wise rider will walk around on foot and determine the best path to take after looking at it from all angles. Know beforehand and memorize exactly what each particular patch or area you are going to work on has to offer and what each rough section comprises so that when you are ready to ride you can concentrate entirely on your riding.

Much of this pre-determination explains the art of riding. Each individual will interpret what lies ahead in terms of what challenge that section has to offer. As an artistic rider you learn to define wisely. Look around and remove manually any dangerous tree branch or rock outcrop that will put an end to your effort and damage your bike if you swipe it. It is wrong and dangerous to blast across un-examined ground, yet it spells failure to take soft ground slowly. Warm up your engine again, after standing idle and getting cold, to obtain hard-working temperature before attempting to negotiate rough terrain.

A tire pressure gauge and hand-pump should be along with you on all trail riding trips. For mud and sand deflate your tires so there is just enough air to support your weight-load without damaging the inner sidewall. Have the tires so they mold like a paw to the traction points. Remember when you are riding out there, not to over-strain the traction points either by abrupt braking or by rapid acceleration. To cross soft ground (with the exception of water which we will study later) ride fast. Stand on the footrests to lower your weight to the utmost, grip the sides of the tank with your knees, and let nothing budge you

ADVANCED RIDING

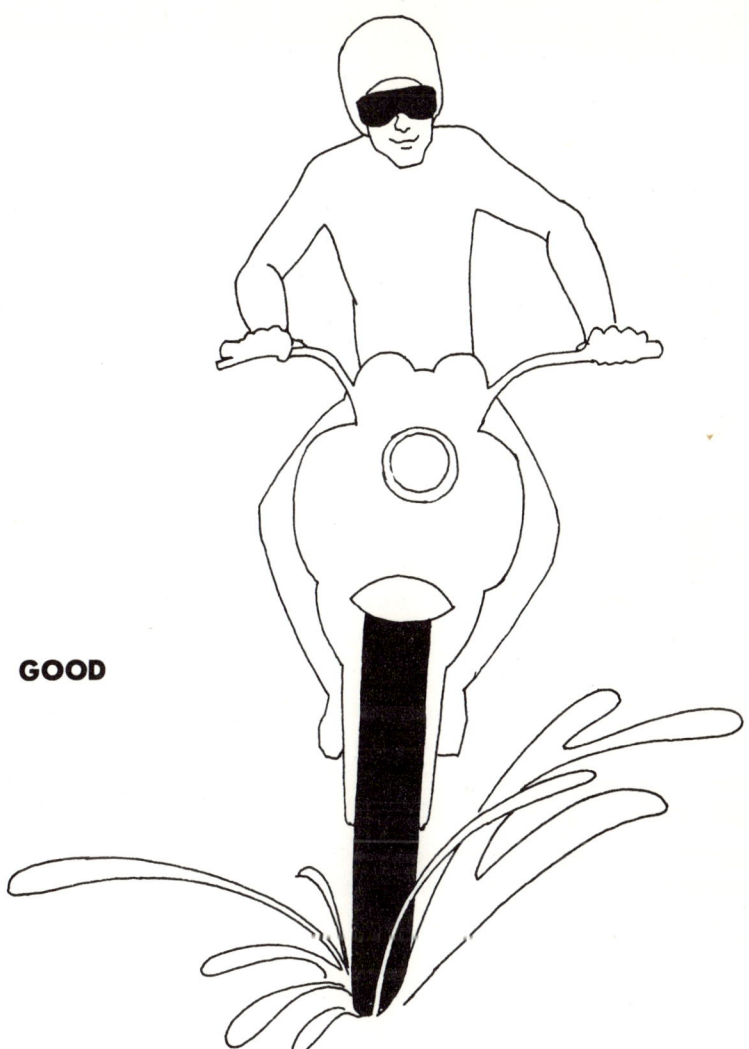

GOOD

Try not to splash as you cross water.

as you skim through. You will perhaps dab a foot first time, but try to stay with it and keep your feet on the footrests, no matter how you slither about. Pick your own path away from tracks where anyone else may have ridden ahead of you and made the surface even softer.

ADVANCED RIDING

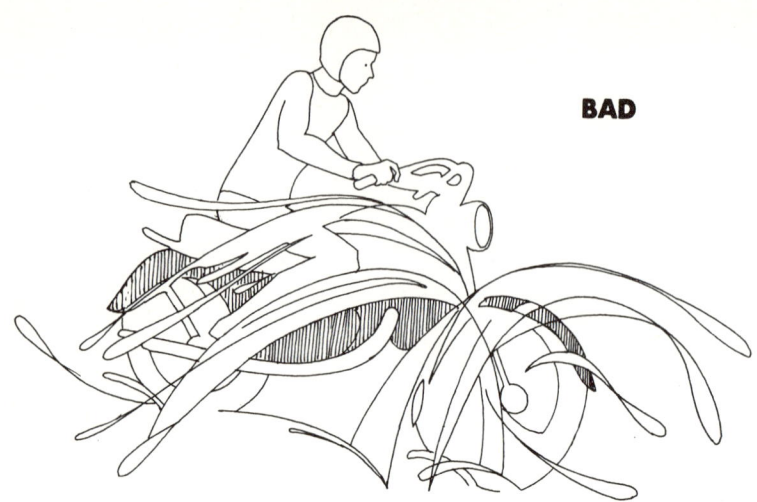

BAD

A hot engine can be damaged if too much cold water is splashed up on it.

After a storm, quite deep water is often encountered as streams overflow or—much more likely—you will find street flooding at an underpass. Hub deep water should not stop you if you do handle it correctly. Be quick to pick the most suitable entry place and pre-determine your "landing-ground" so you are not blocked by a curb or slippery bank to climb and thus be unable to get out of the water. You have to decide several things correctly the first time if you want to avoid engine failure in mid-stream.

Water should be crossed slowly without making a splash. A hot engine can be severely damaged if suddenly immersed in cold water. Try to enter without making a bow wave. Flowing water will dam up against you unless you steer a course slightly "downstream" with the current. Increase the engine revolutions to prevent water from entering the exhaust pipe(s). A well-warmed engine will vaporize slight spray that might splash over it and there is a good chance that high revolutions will spin water out of the ignition system. To do all this, you will need

ADVANCED RIDING

to "slip the clutch." It will probably be only a short distance across the flood patch and the clutch will not suffer by a brief period of what would normally be regarded as abuse. Nevertheless, it is necessary to slip the clutch and race the engine to make the slowest possible headway through water. Usually the ground beneath the deeper part of the water is more firm and gives better traction than the shallow edges where the water has drained away and made the ground soft or slick. Stand upright on your footrests to keep your weight below axle level and imagine yourself prac-

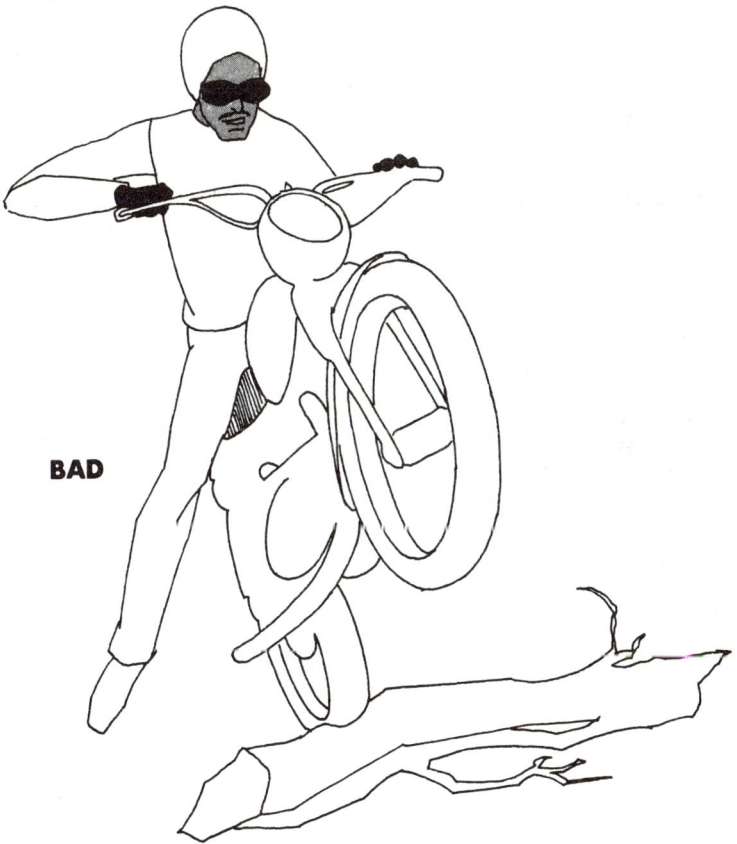

BAD

Never try to force your way over an obstacle. Approach slowly and push your front wheel over the barrier with persuasive power.

ticing for the slow race in next week's field meet. You never thought that you could feel so confident and ride so well.

Stony ground is not so difficult because there is always some grip. Here, it is up to you to do the best you can to get along. Tire pressure must be harder than for soft ground like mud and sand. Know where your traction spot is. Practice so that you can come to a halt with your back wheel exactly on target such as a small piece of paper. In other words, know your wheelbase. It is necessary to be able to work your twistgrip just when the traction point is where you want it to be. Think quickly because there is a little time for putting your thoughts into action. Push your front wheel over an outcrop at close range more by persuasive power (de-clutch/clutch) than by sheer impact. Keep your feet "up" as always and hold the tank firmly with your knees so you do not get bumped off. On stony ground, keep to the track and steer along the path where others have gone before you. Close down the twistgrip if you feel the back wheel become airborne, so the engine will not over "rev" and spin the wheel so fast it will skid when it comes down.

Sports pictures frequently show a competition rider with one foot "down"—usually in soft ground. This is a style of riding which requires a protective steel over-shoe to control power-sliding. Dirt-track riding has a different technique and requires a special kind of machine. So do not be misled because the rider in this instance has a foot on the ground. Keep your feet up on the footrests and learn to handle ground surfaces at the traction point (rear wheel) so you can respond quickly and correctly. Master the fundamentals of riding through mud and sand (soft ground); rocks and outcrops (hard ground); and floods and streams (wet ground), until you get the know-how for each different condition. Soon such road hazards as wet, fallen

For dirt-track competition riding, you need a special steel over-shoe before you can put your left foot down to control a power-slide.

leaves and soft sand at a corner will be approached with confidence and negotiated safely. Think about your style for there will not be anybody to go over the good and the bad points for you.

A measure of your ability is the skill with which you tackle a particularly bad patch. When you can

The special protective steel over-shoe needed for power-sliding in dirt-track competition riding.

ride well enough to get through and over obstacles without having to examine them first, you will be able to take anything in your stride. With experience you will ride well enough to enter in competition and see how good you have to be to win a trophy. At this stage there is no need to refer to styles and forms of famous riders or the merits of their respective techniques. Without the fundamental insight, there can be no real appreciation of good riding.

The International Governing Body of motorcycle sport does organize events in various countries where top-rank factory riders challenge each other in different types of competition. Grand prix road-racing events, trials riders and moto-cross riders have prototype machines and are sponsored by each manufacturer's official competition department. Professional riders sometimes adopt new ways that are especially informative to technicians. Apart from the types of machines, their distinctive styles of riding are interesting to watch and attract many thousands of spectators. Without the enthusiastic effort of factory and rider alike, your motorcycle would never have become the engineering speciality that it is.

11. DIMENSIONAL RIDING

The joy of motorcycling lies in not having any built-in movable mechanical controls between you and the laws of physics. When you are astride your motorcycle, you are right there—in a good riding position to affect your own control. The act of riding is to be in harmony with the laws of physics, which are three-dimensional. For our purposes, we can call these the Laws of Motion, Gravity and Centrifugal Force.

When learning to ride, the beginner must first know what to expect from himself and how he personally reacts to the mechanical controls. Secondly, he must find out what to expect from the machine itself—how the controls respond when he operates them. "I didn't expect it to do that!" is not much help when it is already too late. Only after a while does the learner begin to "feel" how to ride, to "feel" the effect of himself upon the bike apart from the controls, and to be able to understand it and deal with it.

Learning to ride is like learning to read. At first, the beginner does not understand what he is reading; he is only able to make the sounds of the words, but does not know what they mean. Similarly, the beginning rider must try to understand the situation as he tries to manipulate the cycle, and one day, he will finally realize what he is actually doing as he rides. There must be a depth of understanding that goes beyond the mere handling of the mechanical controls. Otherwise, it is dangerous to be on a motorcycle. Simply stated, many "riders" are not riding.

The three-dimensional laws of physics are: the Law of Motion, effective in the horizontal straight path; the Law of Centrifugal Force, also effective in the horizontal plane, but at right angles to the straight path;

and the Law of Gravity, effective vertically. All three dimensions, or vectors, are related, just as the three sides of a triangle are related. If one side or one angle of a triangle is changed, it will affect the other sides and angles. The riding vector, the resultant of the effects that each Law will have upon the other, is what makes the manoeuvre as a whole. Motion, Gravity, and Centrifugal Force bear upon each other in such a way as to be interdependent, the Laws operating on a "give-and-take" basis.

Like all vehicles, a motorcycle is evenly balanced only when travelling in a straight line. Having a single track, a cycle does not possess another set of wheels to take up the imbalance when turning to one side or the other. Nor is it able to go below the horizontal path like an airplane, which can dip its wings or drift.

The Law of Motion manifests itself as inertia—the tendency of an object to continue moving at the same speed in the same direction. The rider can thus become locked onto a collision course, unable to get away from it unless that specific force (as dictated by the Law of Motion) is quickly and drastically reduced. This should be obvious and simple to understand. Nevertheless, it seems that some people get astride motorcycles only to forget the laws of physics and become "laws unto themselves."

Centrifugal force also acts in the horizontal plane, but it is the force that diverges from the straight path. It is really just another aspect of the Law of Motion. If the wheels of your bike suddenly lost traction (skidded) while rounding a curve, the Law of Motion dictates that you would continue to move in a straight-line path. This path would carry you farther and farther from the center of the curve. You would thus sense inertia as a force that tends to pull you towards the outside of the curve. It will therefore affect balance and have an influence on steering (line). Centrifugal force puts an imbalance on one side or the other of the

DIMENSIONAL RIDING 91

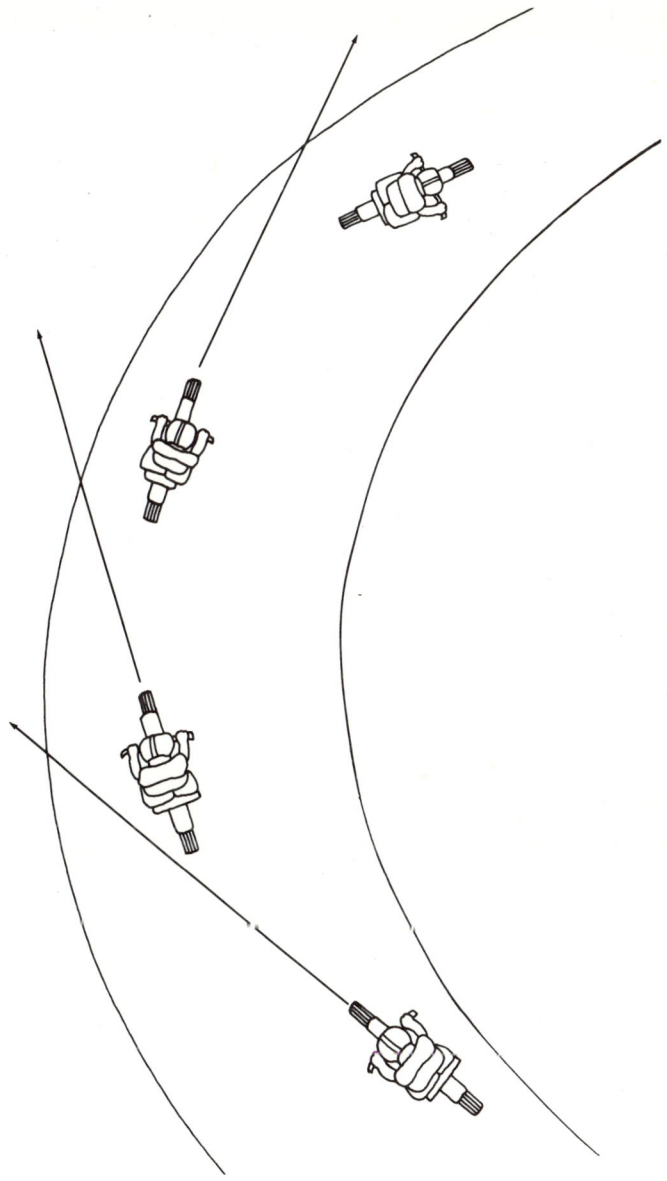

At each point along a curve, the Law of Motion dictates that the rider-motorcycle unit has a tendency to continue moving in a *straight line*. This tendency is perceived by the rider as centrifugal force, pushing him outwards from the turn.

center of gravity according to the direction of the turn —to the left of the straight path in a right-hand turn and to the right in a left-hand turn.

Gravity, or weight, is effective in the vertical path. Weight and friction (traction) are related. The friction of a heavy object resting on a surface is greater than that of a light one. Conversely, when there is no weight, there is no friction—no traction. Gravity also puts an imbalance on one side or the other of the center of gravity according to the direction of the turn, but in a manner opposite to that of centrifugal force. It is a force that pulls one rounding a curve to the inside of that curve, operating in a downwards path to the left of the c.g. in a left-hand turn and to the right in a right-hand turn.

Unlike fixed-load vehicles that have built-in ways to handle them, a motorcycle is controlled, to a certain extent, by rider-function. The dualseat and footrests are a rider's fixed controls. Knees held firmly against the sides of the tank hold the rider in seat center-line. In the straight-line path, whether one sits forward or rearward depends on the speed of the cycle. The farther forward, the closer is the rider's center of gravity to that of the vehicle. This is especially important in a corner or turn where centrifugal force affects them together.

In the early days, sports riders put a small pad on the fender over the rear wheel in order to increase rear wheel traction. But changing the weight balance in this way proved awkward. The modern dualseat evolved to remedy the situation. It is designed to let the rider move farther back from the motorcycle's c.g. so that he may have his weight over the traction point to increase friction at speed. It also allows the rider to sit in a more forward position to bring his c.g. close to the machine's for greater handling response.

Footrests give leverage and disperse weight as low as possible to the left and right of the center of gravity.

DIMENSIONAL RIDING 93

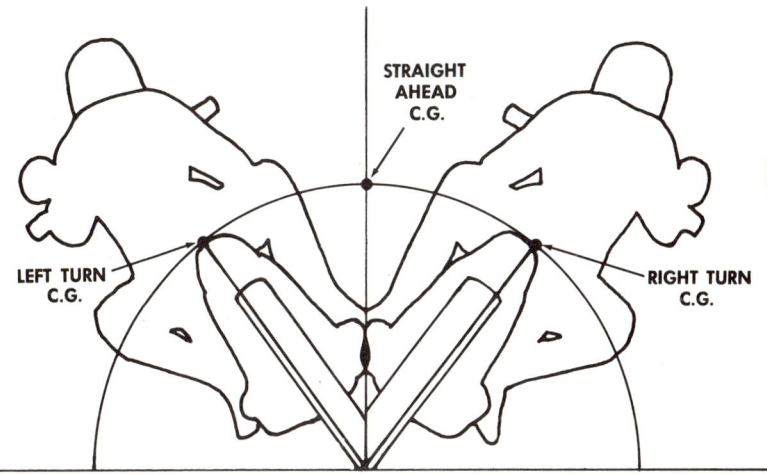

The center of gravity is not a fixed point. As you lean into a turn, the c.g. describes an arc towards the inside of the turn and downwards.

Again, this is especially important for balance and stability in corners and turns. When a foot comes off the footrest and touches the ground while the rider is in a corner, it quite literally upsets things. This action raises the weight applied to the bike to dualseat height and takes it off the traction point, which is already lacking the full force of its vertical vector. Furthermore, thoughtless braking or the inordinately rapid closing of the throttle to slow down causes weight to move forward (according to the Law of Motion) at the wrong time, and can almost completely nullify the vertical force of weight. A chain reaction sets in: loss of the vertical vector means loss of traction, steering becomes off-line and a loss of control results.

Traction and speed are related through what has been called the fourth dimension—the dimension of time. The length of time a particular part of the tire spends on the ground (the traction point) depends on the speed. The faster the speed, the less the time. The stronger the horizontal linear control (the force mov-

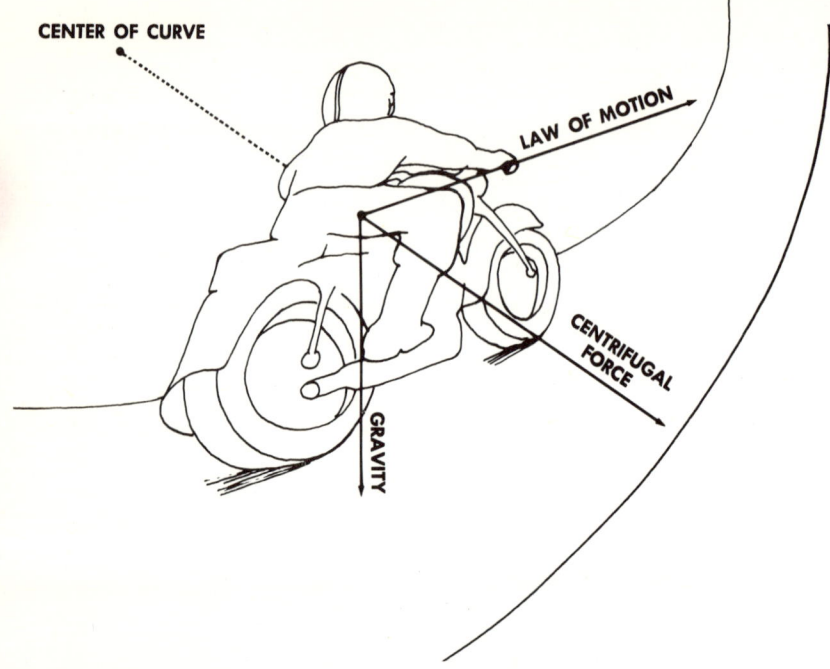

To ride dimensionally is to understand the forces that act on the rider and the machine and to be able to control these forces.

ing the bike forward), the weaker the vertical gravity (weight) friction/traction vector. Conversely, maximum traction exists when there is no motion.

Every action in our lives is influenced by the laws of physics. We take these laws for granted, and say that we are merely employing "common sense." Many people, however, are very thoughtless once they get astride a motorcycle, as is evident by their haphazard or illogical riding positions. They seem to survive by the "Law of Self-Preservation." As one rider said, "I still don't know what I'm doing—I only know where I'm going."

To ride "dimensionally" is to combine all the laws of physics; to be in a state where the Laws of Motion, Centrifugal Force and Gravity harmonize to produce an equilibrium for a particular unit of rider and ma-

DIMENSIONAL RIDING 93

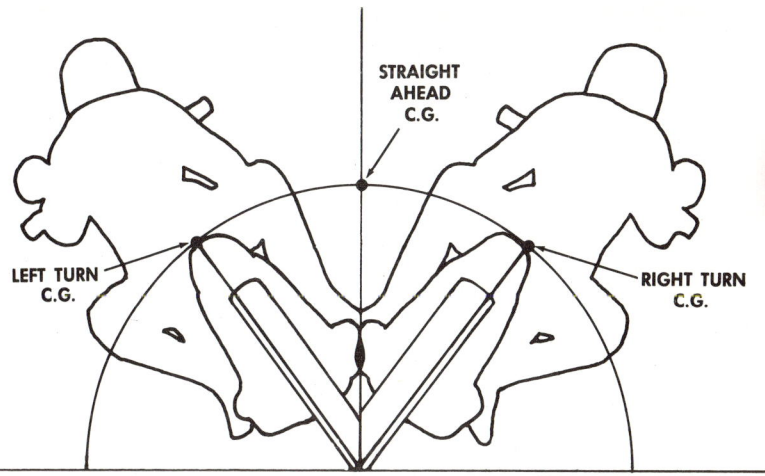

The center of gravity is not a fixed point. As you lean into a turn, the c.g. describes an arc towards the inside of the turn and downwards.

Again, this is especially important for balance and stability in corners and turns. When a foot comes off the footrest and touches the ground while the rider is in a corner, it quite literally upsets things. This action raises the weight applied to the bike to dualseat height and takes it off the traction point, which is already lacking the full force of its vertical vector. Furthermore, thoughtless braking or the inordinately rapid closing of the throttle to slow down causes weight to move forward (according to the Law of Motion) at the wrong time, and can almost completely nullify the vertical force of weight. A chain reaction sets in: loss of the vertical vector means loss of traction, steering becomes off-line and a loss of control results.

Traction and speed are related through what has been called the fourth dimension—the dimension of time. The length of time a particular part of the tire spends on the ground (the traction point) depends on the speed. The faster the speed, the less the time. The stronger the horizontal linear control (the force mov-

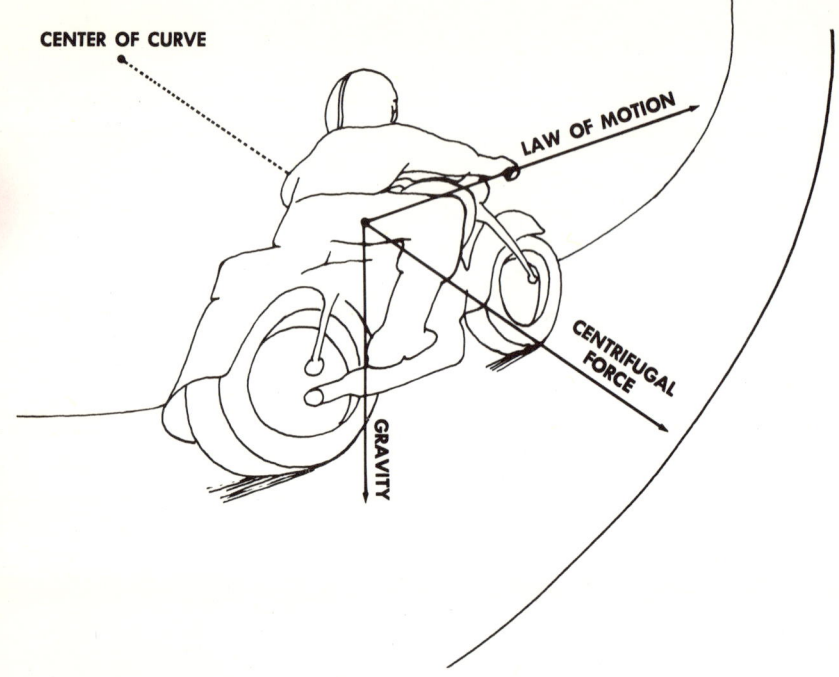

To ride dimensionally is to understand the forces that act on the rider and the machine and to be able to control these forces.

ing the bike forward), the weaker the vertical gravity (weight) friction/traction vector. Conversely, maximum traction exists when there is no motion.

Every action in our lives is influenced by the laws of physics. We take these laws for granted, and say that we are merely employing "common sense." Many people, however, are very thoughtless once they get astride a motorcycle, as is evident by their haphazard or illogical riding positions. They seem to survive by the "Law of Self-Preservation." As one rider said, "I still don't know what I'm doing—I only know where I'm going."

To ride "dimensionally" is to combine all the laws of physics; to be in a state where the Laws of Motion, Centrifugal Force and Gravity harmonize to produce an equilibrium for a particular unit of rider and machine. There is no way to lay a finger on exactly "how" to ride. Cornering and line, braking and speed are all factors of, and ascribable to, intelligent riding.

It takes considerable mileage to gain the experience that will make one a truly proficient rider. But without proper instruction, the road travelled to that experience will likely be a painful one.

The beginner should supplement the know-how imparted by his instructor or this book with his own style. He should be able to feel the laws of physics at work and to take control of them (not ignore them) before they take control of him. He should make allowances for changeable moods or circumstances and to take his time. He will soon discover that he is becoming a safe and delightfully happy motorcyclist.

12. WHAT TO WEAR

As you become more familiar with motorcycling you will know how to select apparel best suited to your individual needs.

From head to toe and from summer to winter, there is a wide selection of practical attire available for every kind of riding. For touring, competition riding, or a short shopping trip, there is motorcycle clothing specially designed for women as well as men. The styles range from serviceable utility wear to fashionable, colorful sport ensembles. The range is so large, in fact, that even seasoned enthusiasts often hesitate before deciding what to buy. Now that you have chosen your machine and have a good idea of how far and how fast you will be traveling, be sure that the riding gear you choose is appropriate.

In some places the law has established certain apparel requirements for motorcycle riding, and it is advisable to check these regulations before you decide what sort of equipment to buy.

Regardless of legislation it is common sense to wear a helmet. Safety helmets come in various shapes and styles to which you can attach a pair of goggles—a peak, a face-shield, or whatever eye protection you prefer. An adequate or "approved" helmet must provide three basic kinds of protection: a hard but not heavy shell to resist penetration; a resilient, energy absorbing inner liner; and a reliable fastening. Care should be taken to see that it is the correct size and a good fit.

Goggles have either plastic or shatterproof glass lenses. As a beginner, it is unlikely that you will be experiencing the high speeds for which the more

WHAT TO WEAR

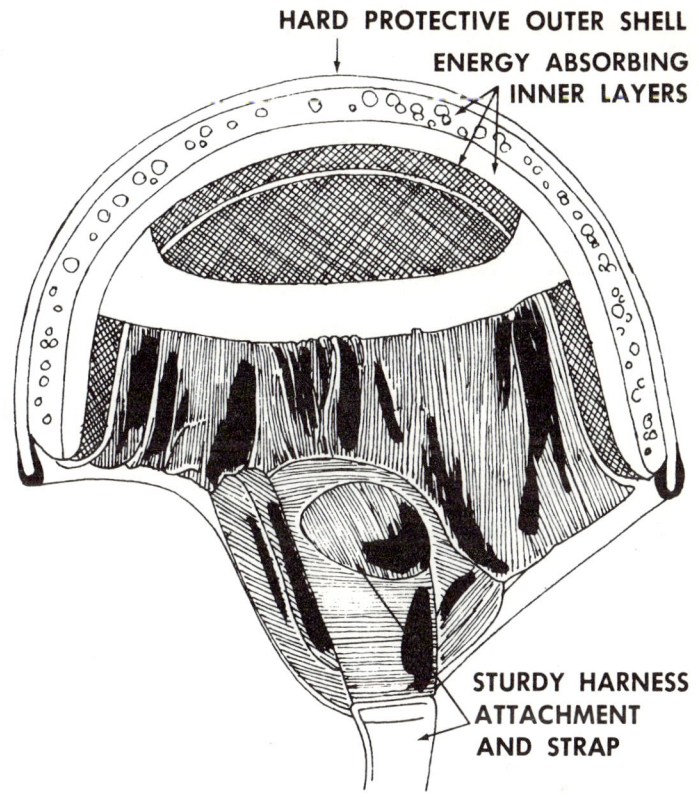

Cross-section of a safety helmet showing the three essential elements of adequate protective headgear.

expensive safety-glass types were perfected. There is a wide variety of less expensive plastic goggles to choose from, including those which fit over eyeglasses. Providing the goggles fit snugly against the rim of a helmet, any of the plastic variety will serve you well. Always wear your helmet when trying on and fitting goggles; otherwise you might find that they do not fit properly when you are riding. The clear-lens goggle or face-shield is the most practical for day—and essential for night—riding. They should be rinsed clean and not wiped, to prevent scratching the plastic.

A tinted replacement lens makes a good spare for riding on a bright sunny day. For winter riding the foam rubber-edged safety-glass type is better ventilated and less likely to mist over and obscure your vision. Face screens and visors, flip-up or fixed, are popular attachments on street and competition type helmets, but unless the frame and strap are stiff enough to prevent twisting they are not very good under wind pressure. When you ride at seventy miles an hour into a stiff breeze, you will have a good idea of what to look for in a pair of goggles or shield. For slower speeds and in cool weather, a handlebar windshield can be very effective.

Even in the hottest days of summer a pair of thin leather gloves to protect your hands is advisable. The grip of fine leather can even improve your handling of the controls and perhaps you already have a pair that would be suitable. When you become an all-weather rider you will find that the short glove is a little drafty and you will need a pair of gauntlets.

The same can be said about the gap at the tops of your shoes. Galoshes or inexpensive plastic over-boots will protect your walking shoes, and you can tuck in your slacks to keep warm, dry, and clean until you decide whether to invest in a pair of riding boots. Sometimes it is more convenient to take off a light over-boot when you get to your destination, than to walk around with boots on. Suitable foot wear is important for the good "handling" of your footrests and kick-starter lever and foot controls. Shoes should not be so substantial that they interfere with your delicate touch on the brake pedal or gearshift lever.

On the whole, your riding kit will depend on the kind of riding you will be doing. Climate and road conditions will largely determine the rest of your apparel. As a beginner there is no need for the full two-piece riding suit worn by professional and experienced long-distance riders. Ordinary outdoor clothes can serve for motorcycling—especially if you already have a leather jacket. Choosing your mount can be an interesting and happy experience, but you have not really finished until you, personally, are safely and comfortably mounted. The cost of good quality riding apparel should be considered and allowance for these extras made at the time you purchase your machine.

When you use your machine for commuting—or to attend that special party—when appearance is a consideration, the nylon or poplin one-piece zip-up coverall is ideal. A large size fitting will leave room to don a jacket or extra sweater underneath if the weather turns cool. These suits are lightweight with snap fastening flaps over zippers, and have elastic at neck, wrists, and ankles to keep out the wind. They come, moreover, in colors clearly visible in traffic.

On a fine summer day you may feel very hot, but once you are going on your bike, the wind temperature will rapidly drop. This natural air-conditioning is very pleasant, but the wind chill factor is something you should think about. It is always advisable to wear a thin nylon jacket.

Sooner or later you will get caught in the rain and wonder about the best way to keep dry. Most rainproof and water repellent garments are intended for walking in the rain instead of forcing your way through it. Therefore, when you buy a two-piece suit or a ventilated one-piece overall, look carefully for welded seams and plenty of overlap covering on pockets and openings. A hand towel worn as a neckscarf will absorb any rain which gets in at the collar. Check to make sure that snap fasteners, jacket zippers, and helmet strap are all secure before you move off so that your neat riding is not spoiled by untidy ends flapping in the breeze. The best helmet in the world is of little value if it does not stay on your head. If you are proud of your motorcycle and the way you ride, it is natural that you should want to look your best. This does not mean you need be expensively attired. Motorcycle enthusiasts are perhaps more clothes conscious now than they used to be. Clothing manufacturers are aware of the growing popularity of motorcycling and their bright, light colored, abrasion resisting fabrics, and their thermal and waterproof materials all contribute to the safety and comfort of your summer and winter motorcycling.

13. YOUR FIRST NEW MOTORCYCLE

Your first motorcycle will be the most significant. For this reason buying your first motorcycle ought to have the same careful consideration that goes with doing anything for the first time. Shopping is very much part of your daily life and every time you buy something, you ultimately depend on yourself to make the right choice. The more clearly you understand what you want, the more likely you are to be right. Choosing your first motorcycle should be no different. In this instance, it is very much a matter of whether you really understand all the facts.

The motorcycle trade offers an immense amount of literature and pamphlets about different models and much additional data can be found in advertisements and road-test reports. There are magazines and publications devoted entirely to what is new in motorcycle development, but these might only increase your confusion. You have very likely collected pamphlets and read about all the up-to-date particulars of the most feasible current models. By the time you have sorted out the preferable points from the less favorable ones, you may still not be sure of what to get.

While still a beginner, you have a special problem. In some places the law restricts the engine capacity for beginners in the younger age group. This law penalizes some riders, but a beginner of any age might really consider getting a small machine to serve merely as a means of finding out, during the first few months of ownership, what sort of machine will actually match his ability. At the same time he can be learning to be a good rider. In the first few weeks, he will become acquainted with the small model, and the strangeness will soon pass. Then the little engine gets overworked and before long the small model becomes a trade-in with a consequent loss of money because of early depreciation. You have to gain experience somehow, and so the value of a machine cannot be thought of in terms of money only. What is experience worth?

Some beginners go to the other extreme and buy a machine that is too powerful. It is a mistake to believe you ought to have a big machine and risk trouble by having more than you have learned how to handle. A big machine can actually hamper your learning because the high speed of which these models are capable is impractical without experience. High speed is the range in which the big machines perform so beautifully, but such speed is pure risk until you have mastered the fundamentals. In the case of long-distance touring, where you really require a large capacity machine, then buying a big bike might be justified. Allow yourself time to practice with it so you can handle it safely. If you want to be the fast and far rider, then buy a machine that will stand up to this kind of riding.

A machine which is intended for the city and short service runs will not be suitable for a long journey. To decide exactly what you are going to use your motorcycle for is not so simple as it seems. Even then, the machine might not always be used exclusively for the purpose for which you first bought it. It often happens that the owner of a highway cruising machine has a friend with a small sports machine he uses for one day endurance competitions. Riding together can be a trying experience. Fortunate is the rider who knows what he wants, gets the most suitable motorcycle for the purpose, and then enjoys it to the utmost within limits.

Despite the perplexing number of models available, the most suitable mount for you must soon be decided so that in the coming days it can play a real part in making your transportation and leisure more enjoyable. A motorcycle shop is almost as good as a motorcycle exhibition and the salesman there will be glad to explain various features and answer your questions. What is the best kind of power unit for you? Two-stroke or four-stroke? Single cylinder or multi? Many enthusiasts who have been around bikes for a long time make comparisons and argue the merits of different machines. Sports reports and racing results are of special interest in this respect because of the particular facts that competitions reveal. Different types of machines vary in character and it is as important to know your motorcycle as to know the character of people around you. Again as a beginner, you are at a disadvantage in this respect because it is necessary to be able to ride quite well to recognize these points.

All machines today are much more efficient and reliable than those of even a few years ago. The modern trend has been to develop models with higher performance and lower engine capacity. Some manufacturers specialize in lightweights and economy models, while others make only super-sports or high-power touring mounts. Think over your requirements honestly and check your reading material carefully. Give particular attention to the more popular makes. There may be a dealer not very far away from where you live who has a stockroom of spare parts and a good service workshop.

A new motorcycle has a list price and so you can be assured you will not be overcharged for it. It is also a guaranteed vehicle. If there should be anything wrong, then repair will be taken care of under warranty. The manufacturer takes all usual and reasonable precautions to assure the quality of material and workmanship. For a certain length of time after you buy your motorcycle, the manufacturer will be responsible through the dealer for all mechanical failures and defects. This coverage also includes components such as tires and the electrical equipment made by each of their respective firms. Although the warranty does not pay for neglect or misuse, a good dealer will spend a great deal of time without additional charge to help you before feeling that he is being imposed upon. After-sale service such as warranty and good will in general can attract you to a place to buy, as much as what to buy.

The list price of the new motorcycle is only part of what it will actually cost. The delivery price is increased by the cost of freight forwarding from a sometimes far-distant land. Machines arrive from overseas in crates to occupy minimum cargo space as well as to protect them and must be uncrated and partly re-assembled when they arrive at the dealer's shop. Each machine is carefully prepared and tested, including a final road test, before delivery to a customer. There is a service charge for that work. The service fee is set by the import distributor. To this sum is added taxes, if any. Therefore, when you inquire about the price of a certain machine, make sure what that figure includes. Summarizing, the delivery price of a new motorcycle unless in close proximity to the factory is about 10 per cent more than the advertised list (F.O.B.) price.

When the time comes to take delivery of your new machine, your dealer will supply whatever special information is necessary for you to know. Be sure that you have your owner's instruction manual and your tool kit.

It will be a great occasion when you first start up your own motorcycle. The "running-in" process is the most important period in the life of your engine. It will be about two thousand miles before a four-stroke, multi-cylinder is ready to perform with full efficiency. With a two-stroke or small single-cylinder machine there is not the same amount of surface area of new metal as there is with a big twin engine and the parts do not require quite so many miles to rub down. During this period your motorcycle should not have excessive loads caused by going too fast or too slowly in the wrong gear. If the engine is allowed to "rev" too high in low or in any gear or labors in a higher gear, then the roughness of the new metal may cause the lubrication to fail with risk of seizure or other trouble from overheating. Rapid or jerky handling of controls is bad for absolutely every component from tires and chains to engine bearings, not to mention your nerves. You must find some way to overcome stiffness without being jerky. Each engine part should be gradually subjected to increased work-load and higher temperatures gently and smoothly until all metal particles have been cleansed away by at least one complete oil change. You must be quick to know if something is not quite right. Providing your new engine is kept turning over lightly and easily, then slightly higher running-in speed if you are going downhill or heading leeward (wind from behind) will do no harm. Motorcycles these days are of good quality and well made. Any dissatisfied owner of a particular make ought not to blame the manufacturer because he is constantly having trouble. If the truth were admitted, the explanation is probably because he did not take the trouble to run it in well. The long-term satisfaction that you will have from your new machine, even under the most demanding and rough conditions later on, will depend to a great extent on how well you take care of it now.

 The selection of your first motorcycle may still be undecided, so if your intuition has not motivated you, then try to be even more objective. Consider your final choice in a three-dimensional way, namely personal, financial, and technical in that order.

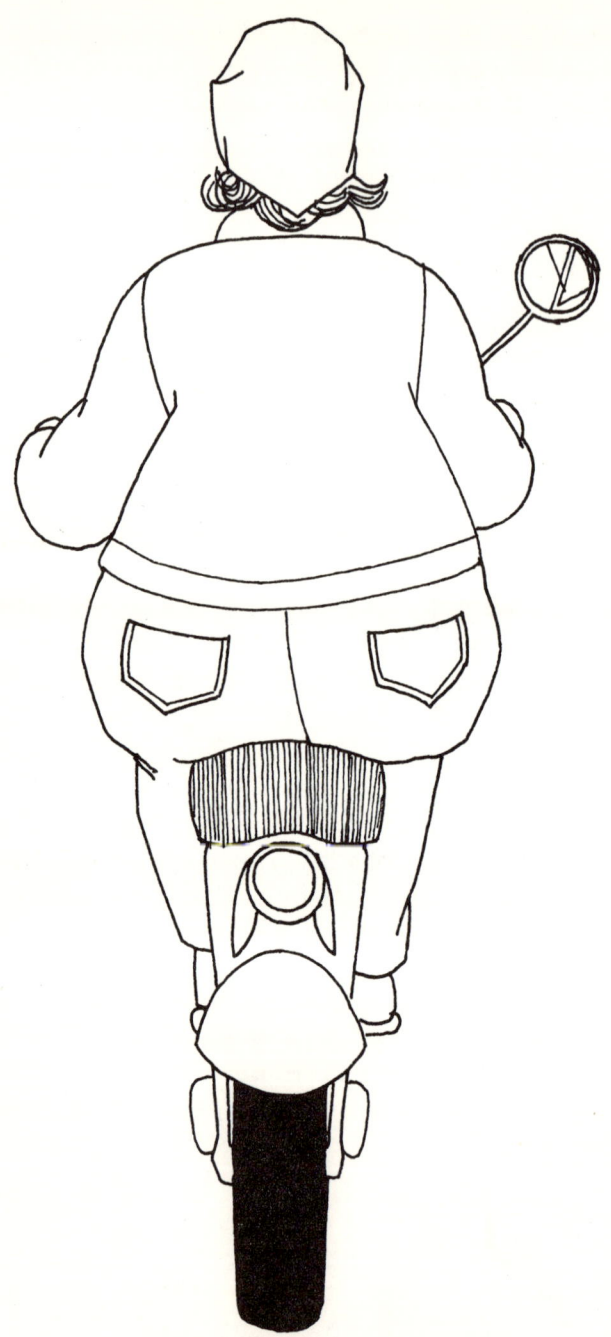

Your bike should fit you.

YOUR FIRST NEW MOTORCYCLE

Personally, you ought to be able to handle your machine comfortably. It should not be too heavy for your size and physique, or conversely, too small a machine for your weight.

Financially, how much money can you really afford? Do you have cash on hand to pay for it in full, or are you able to get credit and finance what you want?

Technically, how many pamphlets now remain in your hand? By now, you have little option left except for choosing your favorite color.

14. YOUR FIRST USED MOTORCYCLE

Probably the first thing you will want to know when you track down a likely used machine is "How fast will it go?" Top speed is not so important, however, as general overall performance. Ordinary acceleration together with good brakes, lighting and steering will be more serviceable and get you about much better. Although the price may after all not have been such a bargain, at least the machine can be depended on to fulfill its purpose without constant repairs before you have some good use from it. There is nothing more disappointing than to miss an enjoyable summer outing because your bike is all apart and you are waiting for spares. A machine in good condition will encourage you to ride better and further and enable you to enjoy longer trips. Whether you buy used or new, the basic question is the same—is this the most suitable one or shall I continue to look around?

If it is possible to find what you want in a motorcycle shop, then surely you will be able to go back there if anything goes wrong or you need some help or more information. This should be a condition of sale. As a beginner you might not be sure of certain points until you come to them and it is advisable that you have a shop to go back to if you have a reasonable complaint.

When a bike is bought from a private party, then you have no recourse if troubles develop. Real bargains arise in emergency situations when a machine is in very good condition, but must be sold because of personal circumstances requiring a quick sale. However, if the model is not the right type, then getting it at a good price is not going to make it right. A usual mistake and quite expensive one is not to realize in time that it is an unsuitable type of machine. It is not always practical to let you have a trial run on a motorcycle as you would be encouraged to do with any other vehicle. The owner does not know your ability as a rider, and since a motorcycle is the only conveyance where the operator is alone at strange controls, the overall risk may be too great. If the favor of a trial ride is offered to you, then be careful not to do anything out of the ordinary.

A trial run on the dual-seat as a passenger will not necessarily tell you what you want to know because the faults are not likely to be demonstrated. It is necessary for you to feel everything for yourself and you will discover that a used motorcycle is a very difficult thing to buy. The most important factors are a true frame and a sound engine-transmission unit. Other essentials are good brakes, lighting and steering. Good appearance is not enough. Indeed, it often conceals all kinds of defects, such as a damaged part newly painted. An out-of-line frame or a cracked cylinder head is more serious than a rough-and-ready piece or wire that you can see is holding things together where a nut and bolt has been lost. You may have to settle for the best demonstration possible under the circumstances and skip the maximum speed test altogether in the interest of safety.

Do not wait until you get home to have a good look at it. Give the machine a careful inspection before it is too late. Get as much information as you can from the present owner (such as the reason it's for sale). Motorcycle appraisal is not unlike any other estimate and will always incur a certain amount of doubt. An experienced rider can, however, tell a satisfactory machine from one with too many faults in a few moments. On a motorcycle almost every part is vital. A motorcycle mechanic could estimate the value for you much more accurately, for with your lack of experience, some quite obvious faults might not catch your eye. General neglected maintenance you will notice. There are some things, however, which even a mechanic can miss. Check to see whether the engine number is the original and if the engine or frame has been exchanged for any reason. Examine the appropriate papers to see if the numbers coincide and if it is legally owned and free from financial lien.

While you are checking the documents and doing the paperwork which in reality consummate the sale, remember to get the owner's manual. If the original book has been lost and is not with the machine, you will be able to get another from the dealer. The owner's manual is not a repair manual, but simply a handbook of adjustments, clearances, lubricants, and details about correct upkeep and general maintenance for normal operation of that particular model. These details may seem obvious, but it is quite easy to get engrossed in the machine and overlook something you are definitely going to need.

As you will see, there are other things to take into consideration that would not apply if the machine were new. Would you consider doing any repair work? Any machine can be made better if you are interested in working on it. Do you have mechanical aptitude and can you undertake to do this kind of work yourself? If you have a little mechanical knowledge and like to work with tools it is an advantage. Many owners like to make motorcycling their pastime and work on their own machines. The pleasure of daydreaming and polishing your bike and adjusting it can give you as much fun and satisfaction as actually going for a ride. Later, you may want to do all your own work and you will learn how to do it after you have actually owned a machine for a while. Eventually when you know how to tune it up yourself, you will find how much this goes hand-in-hand with good riding. When you know the various parts and under-

Polishing and adjusting your bike can give you satisfaction.

stand how they work and have attended to all this yourself, you will have a much better feel for your machine.

When examining a used machine, distinguish carefully between what is maintenance and what is repair or overhaul work. How much of what needs to be done should be taken to a skilled mechanic at a motorcycle shop? At the back of your mind, be thinking about this as you examine a machine. It is useful to take notes about points as different owners explain their machines to you, and make comparisons afterward.

You should be cautious about how many owners a machine has had, and whether some amateur mechanic has tinkered with it. Many machines are obtained for off-the-street riding and intended especially for competition. Occasionally an enthusiast becomes guided by his creative instincts to modify his street machine until it becomes a crossbreed. It can look very attractive to the unwary (and to the one who shaped it that way), but it may not necessarily be a sound engineering proposition and will be absolutely unsuitable for a beginner at any price. Inquire about alterations that may have been made which you cannot see, such as the gearing, the compression ratio, or the carburetor. Is the machine, in short, a standard model?

Until you have learned more about motorcycles, keep to a known and popular make and check into the parts and service situation which is just as important as with a new machine. The most complete appraisal that can be given to any machine has been painstakingly compiled in the following chapter from many years of commercial and competition workshop experience. Take plenty of time before you make your final decision to buy a used bike and use this same systematic method that a skilled mechanic would to check it over.

The best time of the year to buy a used motorcycle is in the fall or winter when the price is lower because of seasonal variations. In areas of the country where a severe winter lies ahead, the present owner will want to sell it rather than let it stand and depreciate and have to service it himself next spring. During the summer a good bike is hard to find at any price so you may have to reconsider buying a new machine. The district or distribution area has something to do with sales. The market varies to the extent of having a reasonable selection in one part of the country and not much in another. The make and reputation of the manufacturer will influence market value. There are, of course, more used cycles sold than new ones and a machine that has been well cared for by only one owner is very likely to be in better condition than one of that same year which has changed hands several times.

What do you expect from your machine? You should expect reliable easy starting, a smooth, fast

YOUR FIRST USED MOTORCYCLE 113

warm-up, and quiet and even operation at all speeds and with all loads. Your motorcycle should give you trouble-free service with normal use for a reasonable mileage. Choose carefully, and in later years when you are still riding and you reflect back, you will truthfully be able to say, "It was a good little bike that I started with."

15. HOW TO CHECK A USED MOTORCYCLE

Whether you want a motorcycle for running around close to home or for venturing on a long journey, it should be in good condition and safe in every respect. A good rider keeps his machine in good order. Loud exhaust noise and hit-and-miss ignition or incorrect carburetion will make it impossible for even an expert to ride well.

The following items should be examined to determine the amount of work and money that you will have to spend to put a used bike into good condition. The availability of parts and the time needed to install them will help you decide whether the machine is worth the price.

Every item listed is not necessarily on a particular machine. A model with a magneto, for example, will not have an alternator. As a non-technically minded individual, you need not delve into mechanics, but the listing should prove a helpful guide.

The check list is arranged in alphabetical order and intended to inform the inexperienced buyer who must take the responsibility of making his or her own purchase. The following items are discussed:

CHECKLIST

1. Accessories
2. Air Filter
3. Alternator
4. Appearance
5. Battery
6. Brakes
7. Cables
8. Carburetor
9. Chains
10. Clutch

CHECK A USED MOTORCYCLE

11. Contacts
12. Controls and Levers
13. Engine
14. Footrests
15. Frame
16. Front Forks
17. Fuel Taps
18. Fuse
19. Generator
20. Guards
21. Handlebars
22. Horn
23. Instruments
24. License and Documents
25. Lights
26. Locks and Keys
27. Lubrication
28. Manual
29. Modifications
30. Mufflers
31. Nuts and Bolts
32. Price
33. Road Test
34. Rubbers
35. Seating
36. Shock Absorbers (Rear Suspension)
37. Spark Plug(s)
38. Spokes
39. Sprocket
40. Stands
41. Steering
42. Storage
43. Switches
44. Technical Data
45. Tires
46. Tools
47. Transmission
48. Voltage Regulator
49. Wheels
50. Wiring

1. ACCESSORIES

An accessory is any item which has been fitted to a motorcycle that was not listed as standard equipment when the machine was new.

The value of a machine can be increased by the addition of extras, but the splendor of an additional chrome luggage carrier and saddle bags and indicator lights should not detract from the issue. Is the motorcycle which is being examined in basically good condition? Check to see that any accessory fitted by an amateur is sound common sense. Chrome ornaments that are sharp objects are dangerous. Brackets that carry a load too far beyond the rear-wheel axle

116 CHECK A USED MOTORCYCLE

A machine fitted with such garish accessories is not only ridiculous but dangerously overladen.

dangerously affect the handling of the machine when laden, and should be corrected.

Enjoy having accessories if you wish, but never let your fervor for these things go beyond a safety point.

2. AIR FILTER

Air filters are fitted to most motorcycles with the possible exception of certain types of competition machines. Check to see that the filter element is inside the air cleaner. Often an owner will take out the filter element on the basis of speed at any price, or perhaps it was clogged and he simply has not replaced it. Unless the carburetor has been re-adjusted, it will cause a weak mixture. It will also indicate that the engine has not been getting the protection from dirt that the filter is supposed to provide. Paper types must be replaced when dirty. Other types can be rinsed clean in a solvent.

3. ALTERNATOR

The alternator produces high tension electricity for the engine ignition and also low tension electricity for the lights and horn. A discharged or weak battery is usually the result of a faulty alternator. A defective unit is not usually repaired, but has to be replaced. A stator is an expensive part, so if you find trouble, first check to see if the cause is not simply a disconnected wire. Under normal running conditions, an ammeter or indicator light clearly seen from the riding position will tell you whether the alternator is working and charging the battery.

4. APPEARANCE

There is nothing like a bit of spit and polish to attract attention. It can also distract attention. Appearance is often changed by alterations that were intended to make the machine look nice, yet are bad practice. Modified seats affect the center of gravity and give a bad riding position. The weight of extra clip-on lights can affect steering. Extreme bend handlebars resulting in remote handling are poor style. Sometimes the most difficult things to see are the serious troubles and concealed damage due to an accident. Fresh paint on the frame should be noted with suspicion especially if repair work was done by an amateur. Normal wear and tear can be made good at list price of parts and estimated labor rate, but where faults are hidden, there is no knowing what may be discovered later.

Good appearance means that the original condition has been maintained and the machine looks as though it has been used normally. Components should be according to the manufacturer's specification or as close to catalogue equipment as possible. Good appearance generally means the machine has had an owner who took care of the little things which show overall attention and good sense.

A good used motorcycle is one that had a considerate rider and has not changed hands often. From end to end, the motorcycle should look right to the most critical eye.

A soft spongy tire will have been inflated and take to the ground correctly. No trace of string or wire will substitute for standard nut and bolt security. Cables and fuel line(s) and spark plug lead(s) and any non-rigid item will be tidy and have clearance to prevent rubbing on the hot engine or a flexing part.

Street dirt is reasonable and should not influence your opinion, although appearance is naturally improved when the motorcycle is nice and clean.

5. BATTERY

Of all electrical faults, the battery generally heads the list. A weak battery will not hold a charge and you will notice that the headlight will fluctuate with the engine revolutions.

There are several possible reasons for battery trouble and most are due to negligence. During use, water evaporates and the acid level gets low or sometimes even goes completely dry. Excessive loads either from over-charging or shorts cause internal damage. Discharge can be from dirt and moisture around the outside of the case. Unsatisfactory mounting can cause mechanical damage or a crack from vibration.

A battery should be clean and dry, mounted firmly and standing on rubber. Terminal connections must be tight and clean except for a little grease smeared on them to prevent corrosion. Acid level should be maintained with distilled water (H_2O), to the top of the separators inside the filler plugs, but not to the top of the battery.

A good battery will maintain full rate when subjected to as much output as can be carried. Test with no engine (generator) running. Watch the headlight beam. Run the stoplight and at the same time touch the horn. A strong battery will maintain a steady, bright beam.

6. BRAKES

No one can question the fact that among all safety factors, brakes stand at the top of the list. Brakes should be road-tested to undergo working conditions. Defective brake-shoes especially on older machines then reveal themselves. Either oval drums or greasy linings show up. The latter, for example, often cause fade-out at the last part of braking after the friction material has warmed up and the grease has been brought to the surface. Worn linings will cause a nasty grab when scraping on a rivet head. Squeaky brakes are due to vibration that can be caused by a loose lining (rivet) or dry dust.

Examine brake cable(s) for neglect. A section of cable out of sight may be frayed and fail just when needed most. Proper adjustment should not operate a brake too soon or too late, because the movement of the lever affects the degree of braking. Late models should have a reasonable amount of adjustment still available on each brake. Spin the front wheel and test the action of the right hand lever. Notice exactly how much effort is required to lock the wheel. Wheels should spin without a trace of binding. A brake should be powerful enough to lock a wheel, but be free from grab. The rear brake should feel firm without excessive travel of the foot pedal. Where a brake is stoplight connected, check to see if the stoplight comes on. The brakes can never be too good, but they should at least brake evenly with any given load.

7. CABLES

Control cables are very likely the most often replaced items on a motorcycle. Cables cannot be serviced except to secure an end nipple, but must be replaced by the manufacturer's standard control. Examine closely both ends of each cable if they are accessible. Look for a frayed strand of the steel-wire which comprises the inner cable. If there is any sign of chafing where the inner cable comes through the outer casing, it will soon break. Immediate replacement is necessary because the cable could break at a critical moment. Flexing of the inner cable is what causes it to break. The end nipple should swivel in the lever to prevent it from flexing. Examine the outer casing for damage or kinks which may have pinched the inner cable.

All the controls, with the usual exception of the rear brake (rod control), are cable operated.

Safe and reliable control of your motorcycle depends largely on the condition of well adjusted cables which are the link between rider and machine.

8. CARBURETOR

Dirt is responsible for most carburetor trouble. Bad carburetion very often brings to light a trouble that is due to something else and need not be the fault of the instrument.

The mixture adjustment and the idling screw are easy to regulate. (See owner's manual for complete instructions.) After the engine has become warm, increase the revolutions very gradually to high "revs." Listen to detect hesitation on the way up and especially blow-back when shutting off and rolling back the twistgrip.

CHECK A USED MOTORCYCLE

The carburetor must not leak when left standing with the fuel tap(s) turned on.

Carburetion should be adjusted so that starting is easy and tickover has a slow and steady beat.

9. CHAINS

Almost every motorcycle is chain driven. Driving chains must be checked methodically and periodically for wear because power from the engine is lost through bad transmission.

It is not easy for a beginner to distinguish between simply what is loose and what is worn. When a chain is loose, it can be adjusted. When it is worn it is so loose it cannot be adjusted further. A worn chain sufficiently loose to jump a tooth on the sprocket may result in a jammed wheel and must be replaced.

To check for wear, push the bottom run of the chain upward with one hand until it is taut. With a prod in your other hand try to pick the chain away from the teeth where it goes over the sprocket. If the chain is in good condition it will not lift, but remain snug on its rollers.

The more daylight there is between the chain and the sprocket, the more the chain is worn. The limit of wear is reached when this slackness is equal to half a tooth-pitch.

Examine the connecting link. The closed end of the spring clip must face the direction of chain travel. An incorrectly mounted clip may cause the chain to part, particularly at high speed.

The chain is a most efficient transmission. Any wayside chain breakdown is usually due to negligence.

10. CLUTCH

The clutch is probably the most abused part of a used machine. It is not good for a motorcycle to have endured poor riding habits, and straining the clutch when coming to a halt is one of them.

A road test is the only reliable way to be sure that the clutch is in good condition. Only a bad case of clutch trouble can be detected when stationary. If there is clutch-slip during the road test then be satisfied that you have already found something defective and reconsider your purchase of the machine.

Check to make sure that the trouble is not just a wrong adjustment. The clutch lever must be smooth to operate and have about three-sixteenths of an inch slackness of cable before coming into action. Check the lever for this clearance. Test also, the ability of the clutch to resist compression of the engine by bearing your full weight down on the kick-starter.

The clutch should disengage freely for quiet and even gearshifts. A heavy clutch can be tiresome in traffic. A strong light clutch will contribute much to the pleasure of your riding.

11. CONTACTS

Ease of starting is proof at least for the present, that ignition is in fair condition. Remove the contact-breaker cover for a more thorough examination.

Electrical parts must be absolutely clean. Burned and dirty contact points warn you that the engine will not start easily much longer.

Contact points should be serviced and accurately adjusted. The manufacturer's owner's manual will give particulars of the correct gap and operational data for the particular model.

CHECK A USED MOTORCYCLE

Good running of your motorcycle depends on good ignition.

12. CONTROLS and LEVERS

A motorcycle that is ridden on the street should have a complete set of controls.

Control levers must have the full range of operation and be clear of obstruction, while you maintain a comfortable riding position. The handlebars on which most controls are mounted should be positioned to give the most functional leverage according to their shape or "bend."

Foot levers are adjustable and should be within natural reach of your footrests.

Correct adjustment of levers and controls make them accurate and responsive to operate.

13. ENGINE

The engine is the heart of a motorcycle. Nothing much can be seen from the exterior, but there are a few danger signs.

A machine for sale has very likely been cleaned for your inspection though it may show an oil leak by the end of a road test. Nuts and bolts with rounded corners denote work by mishandled or wrong tools. Screw slots are good tell-tale items. Excessive use of sealing compound at joints shows the work of an amateur.

Ease of starting is an important guide. Engine tone is more easily determined while warming up from a cold engine when clearances are at maximum. This gives only a very few moments to detect any unwelcome noise before the expansion of parts due to increasing heat dulls the notes of warning.

Listen to the engine with your inner ear. A well warmed engine is in the settled state. Then it should respond evenly to the opening of the twistgrip from a steady tickover to higher revolutions. With a four-stroke engine, exhaust smoke is an important indication of engine condition. Look for black smoke when accelerating (mixture too rich); blue smoke on the "over-run" can indicate worn parts.

Finally, after you switch off and when the engine is still quite warm, test for compression. Lack of compression will indicate an engine that is defective or badly worn. A good engine has a hard compression.

Usually, if a two-stroke engine starts easily and has a steady idling speed it is satisfactory, for there is nothing much to go wrong with these simple power units. Clearances are greater with this type, but when it reaches a point of clatter then it is well worn. The exhaust will always smoke because of the oil-fuel mixture. If correct lubrication has not been added to the fuel of a two-stroke engine, then wear may not be the result of high mileage. Since a two-stroke engine is inexpensive to repair and if other items on the machine check out satisfactorily, then a slightly worn engine might still be a good investment if price of the machine is low.

14. FOOTRESTS

Footrests are fixed controls and are intended to bear the full weight of the rider(s) as conditions sometimes necessitate, to obtain the stability fundamental to good riding.

Each foot should be firmly in position on a strong support. A bent or loose footrest will affect riding position and rider-weight distribution. Never lodge a foot on the side of the engine or on an exhaust pipe.

CHECK A USED MOTORCYCLE

Footrest brackets should be adjusted to bring foot operated controls within comfortable reach. Allow natural movement for each foot to touch the rear brake and the gearshift lever respectively.

Stand astride on the footrests as the machine is supported by the center-stand and strain up-and-down on them. If a footrest will not bear your weight, then either it is faulty or the machine is not strong enough for you. Passenger footrests are equally important.

15. FRAME

The frame of a motorcycle must be faultless. The overall frame is comprised of three sections: steering (front forks); main section (engine cradle); and swinging arm (rear suspension). All three units must be in perfect alignment, because the exactness of the single-track line with a motorcycle is paramount.

Set the handlebars to point the front wheel exactly straight ahead. Make your observation from several feet distant from the front of the machine, with one eye lower than wheel-spindle level. Check to see if the back wheel is in perfect alignment with the front wheel. The back wheel can be adjusted by means of rear chain tensioners.

If there is any discrepancy, the fault may be caused by bad maintenance or it might be a serious defect. When the wheels appear to be out of line at all—double track, side track, or off-vertical—it would be advisable to have expert advice.

16. FRONT FORKS

Front forks must give correct damping action. Pump the teledraulic front forks up and down with both wheels on the ground (off the center-stand). There should be no binding. Restricted action is usually the result of an accident. Excessive action indicates lack of maintenance, generally the failure to renew the damping liquid.

Check for oil leakage around the outer covers caused by faulty oil seals.

Check for visual damage and also for correct alignment. See Frame, section #15.

17. FUEL TAPS

Small parts show wear and even a fuel tap has a limit to its useful life.

Can you smell fumes? If there is the slightest trace of vapor, look closely to see where it is coming from. Fiber joint washers and flexible fuel lines are inexpensive to replace, including the entire fuel tap if necessary.

Slow seepage sooner or later becomes a trickle. Leakage will affect any electrical wire or control cable and it is the main cause of motorcycle fires.

Test the fuel tap(s) by turning on and off.

The action should feel quite stiff.

18. FUSE

The electrical system is protected by a fuse of manufacturer's recommended rating. Examine the fuseholder (battery ignition circuit). Check to see that some makeshift object like a nail is not there as a substitute. Always use the specified fuse.

CHECK A USED MOTORCYCLE

Footrest brackets should be adjusted to bring foot operated controls within comfortable reach. Allow natural movement for each foot to touch the rear brake and the gearshift lever respectively.

Stand astride on the footrests as the machine is supported by the center-stand and strain up-and-down on them. If a footrest will not bear your weight, then either it is faulty or the machine is not strong enough for you. Passenger footrests are equally important.

15. FRAME

The frame of a motorcycle must be faultless. The overall frame is comprised of three sections: steering (front forks); main section (engine cradle); and swinging arm (rear suspension). All three units must be in perfect alignment, because the exactness of the single-track line with a motorcycle is paramount.

Set the handlebars to point the front wheel exactly straight ahead. Make your observation from several feet distant from the front of the machine, with one eye lower than wheel-spindle level. Check to see if the back wheel is in perfect alignment with the front wheel. The back wheel can be adjusted by means of rear chain tensioners.

If there is any discrepancy, the fault may be caused by bad maintenance or it might be a serious defect. When the wheels appear to be out of line at all—double track, side track, or off-vertical—it would be advisable to have expert advice.

16. FRONT FORKS

Front forks must give correct damping action. Pump the teledraulic front forks up and down with both wheels on the ground (off the center-stand). There should be no binding. Restricted action is usually the result of an accident. Excessive action indicates lack of maintenance, generally the failure to renew the damping liquid.

Check for oil leakage around the outer covers caused by faulty oil seals.

Check for visual damage and also for correct alignment. See Frame, section #15.

17. FUEL TAPS

Small parts show wear and even a fuel tap has a limit to its useful life.

Can you smell fumes? If there is the slightest trace of vapor, look closely to see where it is coming from. Fiber joint washers and flexible fuel lines are inexpensive to replace, including the entire fuel tap if necessary.

Slow seepage sooner or later becomes a trickle. Leakage will affect any electrical wire or control cable and it is the main cause of motorcycle fires.

Test the fuel tap(s) by turning on and off.

The action should feel quite stiff.

18. FUSE

The electrical system is protected by a fuse of manufacturer's recommended rating. Examine the fuseholder (battery ignition circuit). Check to see that some makeshift object like a nail is not there as a substitute. Always use the specified fuse.

CHECK A USED MOTORCYCLE 127

19. GENERATOR

A good generator will maintain a good battery. An inefficient generator needs to be serviced. Start the engine and check the charging rate. At cruising "revs," the charging rate to the battery should be equal to the electrical load of all equipment. When headlight, stoplight and horn are applied at the same time, the ammeter will indicate neither charge or discharge, but will balance at zero.

20. GUARDS, SHIELDS and BRACKETS

Shields such as chain guards and fenders must cover moving parts of the machine. Any component that is supposed to be held by a bracket will soon fail if not held securely.

Something rattling or scraping as you ride along is not only annoying, but also quite dangerous. An entirely missing guard can make you very dirty. Thump all around the machine with your fist. You should be able to hear if there is anything loose. See if all guards and brackets that belong to the machine are undamaged and securely fixed in position.

It takes a sharp eye to spot a hole where a nut and bolt used to be.

21. HANDLEBARS

Standard handlebars are precisely what the manufacturer intended for proper control. If the original handlebar has been replaced, find out why. If the original was damaged, be on the lookout for further faults. If the replacement handlebar is a modification, the reason for it should indicate how the machine has been treated.

Handlebars are listed in catalogues as an accessory. Sometimes a replacement is cheaper in price than the original or of a different "bend." Whatever the reason for the replacement handlebar might be, the result is not always rational.

A handlebar that is too high or shaped to come too close to the dual-seat can give leverage which may result in oversteering and possible loss of control. The rubber hand-grips have a relationship to the steering center. No replacement handlebar must position your hands where the steering geometry will be impaired.

Control cables also are affected by unorthodox handlebars. Strain on a control cable because it is not long enough when turning into a corner can be disastrous. Unsafe riding can not be justified by the remark, "It was like that when I got it."

22. HORN

A motorcycle is required by law to have a horn. Be sure that the machine is equipped with a horn in working order. Push the horn button.

23. INSTRUMENTS

The machine should have all instruments listed as standard equipment.

A motorcycle is required by law to have a speedometer in working order. If you are out on a road test, take notice of three readings: the speed indicator; the "trip" mileage, or re-set odometer; and the odometer, which shows total miles traveled.

When indoors, check the speedometer by running the engine with the machine supported by the center-

CHECK A USED MOTORCYCLE

stand so the back wheel is well clear of the ground. Engage (bottom) gear so the speedometer drive will set the indicator needle in motion.

A drive cable is not an expensive item and can easily be examined, if the instrument will not work. A drive cable that revolves without result indicates that the instrument is faulty.

A tachometer—if the machine has one—will register when the engine is started. It is an easy item to check providing you remember to look at it at the appropriate time.

The ammeter is discussed in the alternator and generator sections.

24. LICENSE and DOCUMENTS

Title and Ownership: Negotiate only with the legal owner. The sale of a motorcycle and the transfer of documents from one owner to another is a legal procedure. The motorcycle has a "title." Examine the paper carefully before having it transferred into your name—that is to say, provided you are of legal age. Satisfy yourself that the information on the document is an accurate record of the motorcycle you are going to buy. If there is any discrepancy in the engine or frame numbers and general description, then resolve it before you part with your money. It is an offense to sell a stolen motorcycle or one not fully paid for—one that is, which has a lien.

The engine number is stamped on the side or ʻ the crankcase. No other machine manufactuɪ that number. The frame number is usually on a ɪ̠ tube or steering or seat lug. Rubbed over with chaɪ or similar fill-in, the figures can be clearly seen.

When you pay, get a receipt for your money. Obtaining the title does not necessarily give you legal possession. It must be registered at the motor vehicle office with the name of the new owner entered in the space provided.

Motorcycle license: Vehicle license plates are proof that the owner has paid a government road tax, and your motorcycle must have them if you plan to travel public streets. Apply for your own license or transfer the present license number on the numberplate to your name if it has not expired. License plates are not required if you ride only on private ground.

Motorcycle operator's license: An operator's license is required to ride on public streets. When you have learned to ride well enough and have read and understood the highway code, you may apply for a rider's test. Some states require a special operator's license for motorcyclists; others require only a standard vehicle operator's license.

Insurance, optional and compulsory: If you can get full insurance coverage for your motorcycle, take it. In many states, minimum liability coverage is compulsory. Check with your state insurance department regarding both liability coverage and insurance for damage to your own bike, if your local insurance agent cannot provide enough information.

Summary: Three or four certificates are required for you to ride your motorcycle on the highway:
1. Title: evidence of legal ownership.
2. Receipt of road tax: vehicle license plates.
3. Operator's license: evidence that you have passed the state's requirements for vehicle operation.
4. Insurance: optional or compulsory.

Attend to these things carefully and you will enjoy untroubled pride of ownership.

25. LIGHTS

Lights should be operational at the time of your inspection and comply with local law requirement. A headlight that is adjusted properly will light up the road ahead so that either "flood" or "beam" (short or long range) is in good focus.
The very small indicator lights that illuminate the instruments for night riding will not seem very bright in daylight, but they should light up.
The stoplight when well adjusted will synchronize with the brake(s), lighting as soon as the brakes are applied to give fair warning. A badly adjusted brake light illuminates after braking has started—much too late for the motorist behind you to react.
The tailight must illuminate the license plate. The lighting circuit should not be overloaded by the addition of accessory lights except where provision has been made by the manufacturer for equipment such as directional signals.

26. LOCKS and KEYS

As a protection against theft, the modern motorcycle has a mechanical steering lock to fix the handlebars in the full-turn position.
Where there is battery ignition, you will also have an ignition key, and the tool compartment sometimes has a lock and key.
Make sure you receive a full set of keys for your machine. You may be fortunate enough to receive a duplicate set. If not, have an extra set made and put them in a safe place.

27. LUBRICATION

Engine wear can be caused in several different ways and bad lubrication is a needless one.

Oil condition is a good tell-tale sign of engine care. Oil cools a four-stroke engine as well as lubricates it. Low level makes the pump circulate it quicker than the flow can cool the engine causing overheating. External impurities besides those from combustion accumulate in the oil. Oil does not wear out, but it does get dirty. The result is poor lubrication as well as overheating.

Drain out the old oil if you get a used motorcycle which has become your responsibility. Refer to the owner's manual for the correct grades and quantities for engine and transmission.

Lubrication for a two-stroke is by oil/fuel mixture. Whether from a separate container or measured directly into the fuel tank, the two-stroke depends on this automatic lubrication in accurate proportion. Lubricate a two-stroke with the recommended ratio according to the owner's manual.

The owner's manual will also tell what other parts (such as chains, filters, and cables) of your machine need periodic oil or grease for proper maintenance.

28. MANUAL

The owner's manual belongs to the machine and it should be necessary only to ask for it.

The manual will help you to become familiar with the motorcycle and to obtain a knowledge about different parts and their maintenance.

The handbook will advise you about the controls and routine adjustments. Follow the instructions carefully and you will have many miles of safe and happy riding.

29. MODIFICATIONS

A modification is something that has been altered since the motorcycle was manufactured. External modifications are easy to see, yet they are often unknowingly overlooked. Substitute parts such as footrests which are too high or improvised seating should not escape your notice.

Internal modifications to the engine such as oversize pistons affect timing and compression ratio and result in a false impression of the model. Gearing that has been changed may make the machine unsuitable for street riding. A machine with internal modifications should generally be considered in the competition class and therefore unsuitable for normal street and road use.

In the case of an older machine, satisfy yourself by asking whether any modifications have been made. Where modifications have been made, they should be sound design and good mechanics.

30. MUFFLER(S)

Noise is the greatest enemy of motorcycling. Original mufflers are quiet and efficient and emit an acceptable sound level of exhaust.

Noise does not mean that the engine is more powerful. A muffler that has been tampered with and made noisy can adversely affect engine output. Be sure that the mufflers are original.

31. NUTS and BOLTS

Nuts and bolts are fundamental. No item is so sure to spoil the appearance of a nice machine as a slipshod stove bolt.

Glance over the nuts and bolts. Rounded corners show poor workmanship or the use of wrong tools.

Three bolt systems are in current use: S.A.E., English, and Metric. A nut or bolt (or screw) that has been lost should be replaced by another of that same system. Remember that wrenches also must be of the appropriate system.

32. PRICE

There is no list price for a used motorcycle, but you usually get what you pay for. The price of a used machine depends on several factors: its manufacture, year, model, and price when new; its condition; and the locality and season.

Good makes bring the highest prices although a good model that is no longer made will not be worth as much as one in current production.

Small motorcycles depreciate more rapidly than bigger machines because they are more plentiful and less sturdy.

In places where there is year-round riding, the price will not fluctuate as it does in places with extreme seasonal variations.

If you really like the bike and it checks out well in other respects, then you will have to accept or haggle over the final item—the price.

33. ROAD TEST

A short distance is quite sufficient to reveal all you want to know, if the job is done with understanding and when attention is given to all points in systematical order.

No two people ride alike and you might detect a

CHECK A USED MOTORCYCLE 135

vibration or a steering fault that the owner has become accustomed to.

The trial run should correspond to the machine being tested. A ride around the block might suffice for a utility machine but it would be inadequate for a sports model.

Every single detail will not perhaps be noticed in a brief road test, but unless something is quite wrong the overall performance should tell you a good deal about the condition of the machine.

Starting should be easy. The engine should respond well and be free from fussiness. Handling and roadholding should feel light, certain and waggle-free. Lighting and general equipment should be efficient.

Finally—and this is best done away from the machine—assure yourself that the bike is essentially what you want. Is there a dealer within reasonable distance for your maintenance and parts service? Does the motorcycle have a "good nature?" Is it easy for you to ride and do you feel it will please you?

34. RUBBERS

Rubber covers are fitted as standard equipment over footrests, kickstarter, and gearshift lever. Handgrip rubbers are designed to allow good touch without having to grip.

Rubbers may seem unimportant, but they tell their tale.

35. SEATING

Firm seating accommodation is essential to a secure riding position. Dual-seats become torn and come adrift when misused to pull the machine onto the center-stand. Be sure that where you sit is secure and safe.

36. SHOCK ABSORBERS (Rear Suspension)

Many motorcycles are ridden two-up for a big part of their mileage. The additional weight of a heavy passenger may cause a suspension unit to lose effectiveness and the left and right sides to vary.

Strenuous riding over rough ground or accidental damage may have weakened a damper.

A faulty shock absorber will affect road-holding ability, especially on a bad road surface.

Maintenance work might be possible, but usually at least one new unit is the only remedy. Check the left side and right side shock-absorber units by comparison as well as possible, by feeling each one with a shake of your hand.

37. SPARK PLUG

A motorcycle engine, because it is air cooled and has quite a high compression ratio, operates at a very high temperature. The spark plug gets the brunt of the burden. Spark plugs should be the type recommended for the engine by the manufacturer. This is always stated in the owner's manual.

The plug should make a gas-tight seal with the cylinder head and show no trace of oil seepage, yet not be so tightly inserted that it stresses its own internal gas seal.

Removal of the spark plug for inspection of this important part of the ignition system will show not only its own condition, but also that of the engine. If the insulator around the point-gap looks a brownish shade, and not sooty black (rich mixture), or heat white (weak mixture), this is the sign that the spark plug is running at a good self-cleaning temperature and that the carburetor is correctly adjusted.

Finally, the spark plug should have a good, firmly fitted, insulated cover.

38. SPOKES

A bad spoke is an easy and dangerous thing to miss. A faulty spoke may have come to rest behind a chainguard and hidden from view. It will not take long to turn each wheel and look carefully at every spoke.

Bad spokes can be detected by the sound they make when brushing past a pointer held in your hand as the wheel spins. A strained spoke has a high pitch. Loose spokes have a dull sound. Each spoke must take its share of weight yet not be too stiff. A certain amount of flexibility should be allowed if spoke breakage is to be avoided.

See that the wheel-rim runs true. Spoke adjustment is done after the tire has been removed.

39. SPROCKET

The sprocket is a part of the transmission system where power is often needlessly wasted.

Check the rear wheel sprocket if possible where there is no chain guard cover fitted. All of the teeth should be evenly worn on both back and front so as to look symmetrical in shape. Curved or hooked teeth are a sign that the sprocket is badly worn. You should be cautious about a motorcycle whose parts show this extensive wear.

40. STANDS

The ordinary motorcycle is fitted with two stands either of which will support the machine when it is parked: the center-stand and the prop-stand.

Test with your foot the power of the return spring to snap the stand back into place. Never ride with a weak return spring or use a piece of string to hold it up.

On a corner or on bumpy ground it is extremely dangerous for a stand to drop or swing out or to hang low underneath the motorcycle.

So check each stand. See that it lifts well clear off the ground. A machine without a stand is inconvenient, but at least it is safe to ride.

41. STEERING

A motorcycle with well adjusted steering has a lot in its favor. Loose adjustment has a hammering effect as if riding on a rough road. Tight steering adjustment causes swaying or weaving.

When steering is neglected, the taut, precise handling so necessary for tricky patches is impaired.

Check the steering head for tightness or slackness. Loosen the steering damper and feel the bearings with the front wheel clear off the ground. Check for movement between the upper and lower ball races in the steering head. Swing the handlebars from side to side and see whether there is any strain on electrical wiring or on control cables. Besides interfering with the steering, such strain may soon lead to faltering lights or a pinched cable.

Remember, it is easy to notice poor control after it is too late.

42. STORAGE

A motorcycle stored for the winter should be serviced before it is re-started.

Storage does not affect a two-stroke engine to the same extent as a four-stroke type. However, it is advisable first to rotate the engine manually several times with the kick-starter to free a piston ring or anything that may be stuck before actually starting the engine.

CHECK A USED MOTORCYCLE 139

To start a four-stroke engine without manually setting the parts in motion is always harmful. Where dealer workshop facilities are not available, then you must do the service work the same as for a new machine.

The battery should be fully charged and the electrolyte level checked.

Check your owner's manual. It tells you what particular servicing your machine will require before you can put it back on the road.

43. SWITCHES

A headlight dimmer switch that can plunge you into sudden darkness at high speed is disconcerting.

See that the left side handlebar switch will not cling between the beamlight and the floodlight.

Be sure that the brakelight switch is free from road dirt.

44. TECHNICAL DATA

Motorcycles are classified in cubic centimeter capacity (cc.), although the rating is sometimes specified in terms of horsepower.

If you purchase a used motorcycle and the Title is rated in horespower, you will not actually know what size it is. Each manufacturer has a wide range of models and sometimes there is very little external distinction between them.

Check the size of the engine (capacity in cc. volume). The name given to that particular model or its catalogue number will also have the technical data, so there is no possibility that you can mistake one machine for another.

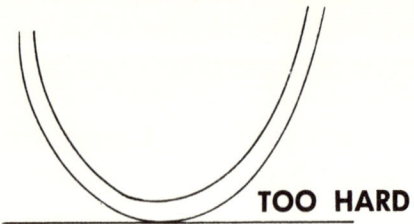
TOO HARD

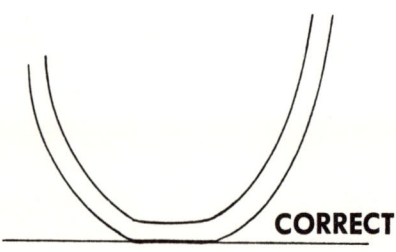
CORRECT

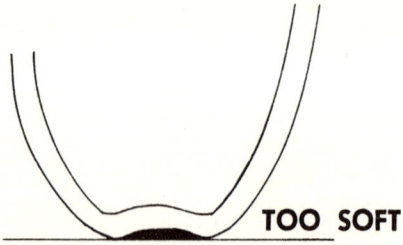
TOO SOFT

For good traction under normal street and road conditions, tire pressure must be neither too hard nor too soft.

45. TIRES

Tires are something that you probably have thought of checking by yourself.

Tires should hug the road surface as if your life depends on it, which it does. Tires with the right tread and pressure will respond to your brakes when you need them, especially on wet roads.

A tire that is too soft can cause considerable instability and invites punctures.

A tire that is too hard decreases the traction area and also affects the pliancy of the tread.

Check the pressures with a little gauge of your own before going out. See your owner's manual for recommended pressures. Tires get warm on a run and this gives a false (high) reading. Public (free) gauges can be inaccurate and for a motorcyclist, this can be very serious.

Worn and neglected tires are particularly dangerous on a motorcycle. Examine them carefully for cuts and damage.

A front tire that has worn unevenly indicates a steering fault.

Check to see that the tires are running true on the rims. When a tire is not mounted properly, it can give the impression that the wheel is out of line.

See that the inner tube valve cap is not missing. The cap protects the core which is keeping the air in. Small pieces of equipment like the valve cap are important and, if neglected, can lead to time-consuming breakdowns.

Good traction has a lot to do with your safety. The quality of tires and tubes was never better than it is today and yet tire trouble is one of the main causes of roadside breakdowns.

142   CHECK A USED MOTORCYCLE

46. TOOLS

A small set of screw drivers and wrenches (including a spark plug wrench) is standard equipment on all motorcycles. If you are lucky, you will also receive with your used machine the small special gauges which are important for correct settings and adjustments of bearings and clearances. These tools are necessary for good maintenance and are the same size and system of manufacture (S.A.E., British, or Metric) as that of the machine.

It is hoped that at least some of the gauges will be included with your machine not because of the money, but because they are a very definite part of your motorcycle.

47. TRANSMISSION

The older the motorcycle, the more the transmission is worn and the greater the tendency for it to "jump out of gear"—especially when accelerating "up."

A road test is the best way to check the transmission. Gearing should be standard ratio. Gearshift lever action should be decisive in all positions and gear-shifting smooth and quiet. The kick-starter lever should engage for its full range to turn over the engine properly, and then spring back. Oil level and consistency of the oil is easy to check if the transmission has a dip-stick.

48. VOLTAGE REGULATOR

The voltage regulator as the name implies, regulates the flow of electricity passing from the generator to the battery. A discharged battery is often traced to a faulty regulator. See Generator, #19.

CHECK A USED MOTORCYCLE 143

Start the engine and watch the ammeter or indicator light. When the ammeter indicates positive, or the indicator light becomes extinguished, meaning that the generator is charging, check for a loose wire or a bad connection. To meddle with a regulator is seldom satisfactory. Replace the faulty one with a new and guaranteed unit.

49. WHEELS

Wheels are important. The front wheel especially so, because it affects your steering. It should spin freely and be well balanced. An unbalanced wheel at high speed can lift clear off the ground on every revolution. Excessive play in wheel bearings affects both braking and steering and is dangerous.

Generally speaking, a wheel with a wobble can be corrected. An oval wheel or one with a flat spot should be rebuilt with a new rim.

Tilt the machine backwards or forwards on the center-stand to raise either the front or the rear wheel off the ground for inspection. Spin back the wheel to see that it is absolutely true—that it is perfectly circular and does not wobble from side to side.

50. WIRING

The harness or loom that contains the wiring is channeled safely away underneath the tank.

Individual wires branch off from the main conduit to make connection with the various electrical components and can be distinguished by a color code (see owner's manual for wiring diagram).

Special ends fit together so the connections are strong, tight and reliable. They are well insulated and secured. It is true that sometimes a connection will come undone, but with a little investigative work you should be able to trace it and repair it, if necessary.

Bend over and glance underneath the tank and see if, instead of being safely in the harness, there is a tangle of separate wires. Frayed wiring held together by one remaining strand or a corroded terminal shows negligence and will soon cause you trouble.

Check places like the steering head where there is flexing of wires and connections that are exposed to road dirt.

Good wiring and tight connections will save you trouble in wet weather or over rough ground.

You will be very pleased when you have at last chosen your motorcycle. In the future, you will have many happy hours of recreation as well as many useful trips.

Ride well—whether you are in the city and commute through dense traffic or travel out in the great wide countryside.

16. PROFESSIONAL INSTRUCTION

Many people would like to ride motorcycles, but they cannot teach themselves. There are too many accidents involving beginners learning to ride. The majority of motocycle accidents and fatalities occur during the first few miles, during the first weeks of ownership. This is both unfortunate and unnecessary. Beginners' reactions and miscalculations when left to themselves are too often the cause of calamity. A professional riding school, not the streets and highways, is the best place for beginners to find out whether or not they are able to learn the art of motorcycling and to do so with the proper degree of safety. The skill and knowledge gained here will ultimately influence the selection of the model and the specifications of the motorcycle the beginner will finally purchase. He will have learned two important things—what to expect of himself and what to expect from a motorcycle.

Teaching motorcycle riding is beyond the ability of a friend who rides, do-gooders, well-wishers, or any other amateurs. For years I had been around motorcycles of all forms and in all situations from commercial and competition to technical and teaching, and believed I really knew how to ride—until I started teaching beginners. Teaching, too, requires experience.

Motorcycle instruction is a professional service. Responsibility for proper training has to be pinned down to somewhere and somebody. There are not enough beginners at any particular dealership to justify a full-time instructor. The salesman reassuringly tells the beginner, "We'll teach you." There is a mistaken idea that if you can ride a bicycle and drive a car, then you can handle a motorcycle. A few minutes to explain the mechanical operation of the motorcycle is often enough to get a signature or a deposit, and the machine is soon being serviced. Hesitation might result in the loss of a sale, and that is not good for business. Dealers are often quite happy to bring the motorcycle to the beginner's home in a truck and drop it off with a cheerful "It's all yours!" The alternative, the beginner riding it home, can be dangerous.

The process of learning to ride a motorcycle, when compared with similar activities, puts the beginner at a disadvantage. Facilities and instruction are readily available for golf, swimming, tennis, football, etc. Car students can apply for a permit and learn with an instructor sitting alongside, using the public streets. Motorcycle learners' permits are not always available and even where they do exist, the street is not the place to learn to ride a motorcycle. The occurrence all too often is for a motorcycle beginner to use an empty parking lot. Unfortunately, the police or the property owner often put a stop to it, claiming trespass on private property. This situation can and should be easily changed.

Motorcycle transportation, which is becoming increasingly more popular, must be given due consideration. Not legislation nor insurance, not the wearing of a helmet nor the standardization of motorcycle controls, not being careful and observing the Highway Code nor "watching out for the other guy"—none of these can prevent an accident if the motorcyclist has not learned how to function. Professional motorcycle instructors are undoubtedly the link between the manufacturer, "the trade," and the acceptance of the motorcycle as an economical and safe means of transportation by the general public.

A riding school is something apart from the mechanics and maintenance of the machine itself. Dealerships have well-equipped service departments

PROFESSIONAL INSTRUCTION

with factory-trained personnel, and there are plenty of mechanics to see that the bike is in good condition.

A riding school should not be overly concerned about the Highway Code and the "Rules of the Road," which are the same for all road users. The majority of beginners are already qualified car drivers and experienced road users. The emphasis of a riding school should be on the dynamics of riding—the relationship between the rider and the machine apart from its mechanical controls.

In the hundred years or more since the motorcycle was first considered to be a roadworthy vehicle and licensed to be ridden on public streets, the subject of correct riding has never been given the attention it properly deserves. And yet, this is the requisite for the safe and enjoyable handling of the powerful and highly developed types of machines that are now on the market.

The best way to teach motorcycling is to teach motorcycling. The difference is great between what a beginner knows he should do once a task has been explained and actually being able to perform that task. A riding school teaches this know-how. It is a tricky subject to teach because a motorcycle is the only vehicle where a beginner is alone at strange controls. An instructor is not able to run alongside nor to shout loudly enough to explain what is happening as the learner moves out of earshot. There is no one with the learner to take care of his blunders or to help with advice before something happens or a wrong action becomes a bad habit. If things are not done correctly in the beginning, that is, if the learner is not properly oriented to the motorcycle, especially as to the effect of his weight upon the vehicle, the odds are that he will not learn the right way until it is too late.

There is a standard way to mount a horse, to get into a boat, and to hold a gun. Similarly, there is a proper way to get astride and be seated on a motorcycle. A riding school teaches standards. Millions of motorcycles are registered in the country every year and the number is increasing, yet individual riders seem to learn by trial and error, and many are doing so with disastrous results.

Book learning is not entirely satisfactory. Schools operate to bridge the gap between plausible theory and the proof of that theory in fact. A motorcycle is not a dangerous vehicle, but without proper instruction, it is dangerously ridden much too often.

A riding school is a motorcycle kindergarten. It is a way to learn reliable and accurate handling of the mechanical controls at slow speed and in low gear, with the emphasis on rider displacement technique. The beginner learns this degree of control before attempting manoeuvres extending it to higher speeds, and only after it is obvious that there is no haphazard handling of the machine.

Exercises are undertaken not for the purpose of building up mileage on a motorcycle or for merely having fun, but to give the beginner an awareness of rider-weight control. The exercises employed in workouts are intended to demonstrate the underlying principle of the lesson being taught. Workouts are for the beginner to learn to regulate his own functioning as a movable, effective control. The important thing is for the learner to concentrate and give his complete attention to what he is doing all the time he is riding. This is fundamental to safety no matter what the vehicle, because only by thinking can the beginner anticipate and act.

The beginner must learn to ride decisively rather than defensively. The rider who is uncertain or who has a negative attitude will sooner or later hesitate at a crucial moment and will find himself in a great deal of trouble. The rider must be thinking of what he is doing at all times—not only when he is starting or stopping, changing gears or riding through high-speed curves.

A good rider is alert, yet completely relaxed. He rides with an efficiently controlled style—a beautiful blend of movement that carries him along both smoothly and unobtrusively.

A good instructor starts by assuming that the student knows nothing about the subject to be taught. "I thought you knew that," is a refrain that is not only unfair to the student, but also represents negligent instruction. The student must prove himself to the instructor, and can do so only if the instructor first assumes that the student knows nothing.

The instructor must also be able to anticipate what type of person will make what type of mistakes and then prevent him from doing so. The ability to do this is enhanced by the instructor's remaining quite alert during the preliminary orientation and simply putting two and two together in sufficient time.

A true riding school is necessarily a two-way institution. There must be a two-way exchange between instructor and learner. If there is no interchange of information, no communication, no feedback, there is no real learning taking place. The course then becomes "Do as I said," rather than "Use the information I've given you and learn to think for yourself." This is the difference between mere *training* and effective *education*.

Completing the course of instruction does not always mean that a student has reached an acceptably safe standard, though some of them are not quite bad enough to be talked out of riding (even if that were possible). These people should be given a few words of caution and advice, especially concerning the type of machine best suited to their needs and abilities.

Undoubtedly, there will be a few students unable to succeed in doing some of the manoeuvres even with the best of instruction. If a student has any talent, it is up to the instructor to develop that ability to the utmost. However, if a student does not have the aptitude, then no one can give it to him. There will, of course, be rejects—those refused admission to the school and those who have failed the course. To those who are disqualified, the message should be clear. Unfortunately, my files contain reports of the fatal accidents of some of those that I have been forced to reject—people who should never have been on a motorcycle in the first place.

There will, of course, be drop-outs. A drop-out is usually someone who takes two workout periods and is still trying to come to grips with the techniques taught in the first period. He has learned how to make the bike start and stop, and then decides to carry on by himself and take to the streets. Unfortunately again, the results are often disastrous.

The most critical element of workouts is the beginner's rate of progress. It is a criterion of how a person might be expected to react on a motorcycle in an actual traffic situation because, once on the street, things must be done right the first time. The workout can be done in an hour. If it is done in less time, it does not indicate that the lesson has been shortened, but rather, that the student was quick to learn. Some things do not come quite so easily to some people. They will have to repeatedly work at each exercise, and will naturally take longer.

A lesson should not last more than two hours. After a while, the student will get tired and begin to make mistakes. The instructor should notice this, and end the lesson before fatigue sets in. A student who runs out of time before completing the day's work may want an extra hour or so. Some students have to be urged along. Some older persons may progress at a slower rate, and some may soon reach the limit of their capabilities. Extra time is advisable for one, and yet almost a complete waste of time for another.

The end of each workout is "free time," with no special assignment, but with time to practice and prepare for the next lesson. Likewise, the beginning of the next workout is "pick-up" time, because it gives the student a few minutes to pick up where he left off. This gives continuity to the lessons, and is also a precautionary measure in case a student has forgotten material from the previous lessons, or has simply lost his coordination. Believe it or not, some people will take the entire period just trying to pick up what they were doing before. These are the ones with limited ability, and it will be that way with them all along. No amount of money, no additional tuition fees, no logging of more time, will make much difference. With few exceptions, anyone who is not able to finish the course in the maximum time of two hours for each of the three workouts should have second thoughts about motorcycle riding.

The best times of the day for workouts depend upon the season of the year and vary with the locale. During the heat of summer, for instance, early morning hours and the long daylight evenings are practical periods. Wintertime appointments will sometimes have to be rescheduled because of bad weather, but this should not prove troublesome since there are generally fewer enrollments during this time of the year. A riding school can operate on a year-round basis. In the eastern part of the country, winter can be a good time for instruction, as quite often the beginner is in the process of purchasing the new year's model and he will want to be ready to ride by spring.

Many persons do not have enough self-discipline to learn the right way to ride, but are, rather, satisfied just to be able to start, stop, and proceed in a straight line. Sometimes the instructor is hard-pressed to know how to handle such a student. Experience in teaching will take care of those situations.

One day, there will be enough good riders to change the public's unwarranted opinion that motorcycles are dangerous. Dependable evaluation of a student's riding abilities is an attribute of quality instruction. It can prevent accidents and save lives. It will ensure that riding schools continue to produce graduate riders of the highest standard.

GLOSSARY

QUESTIONS AND ANSWERS

Q. Why is it important to keep both feet firmly up on the footrests?
A. To maintain control over foot levers. To apply your weight, when desired, to a lower part of the machine.

Q. Which brake is the most powerful, the rear foot brake or the front hand brake?
A. The front brake. Weight moves forward as you slow down. The front brake is designed to take the increased load.

Q. Why is it advisable to use the hand brake when mounting and dismounting?
A. To prevent the machine from rolling while you stand on one leg.

Q. Which foot supports you on the ground when you come to a halt?
A. Your left (gear) foot. The right foot must use the lever to apply the rear brake.

Q. Why is it important to know your tire pressures?
A. Good traction depends on correct tire pressures.

Q. What is an engine?
A. An engine is the means to convert chemical energy (fuel), to mechanical energy (horsepower).

Q. What special care should you take when riding a strange machine?
A. Feel it out first. Different machines even though of similar make and model react differently.

Q. What is meant by "correct riding position"?
A. A firm seat with knees against the sides of the tank; feet securely on the footrests—arms and hands loose and free for accurate control of levers and the handlebar not used as a grab-rail.

Q. Which is your clutch hand?
A. The left hand. The clutch lever is always on the left handlebar.

Q. Where are the two dynamic spots or places that you should bear in mind, especially when in awkward situations?
A. The center of gravity. When the rider moves forward, his weight is shifted to a more central location. The traction point—maximum weight/adhesion (feet up on the footrests to exert full load).

Q. On a wet street, should your tire pressure be harder or softer?
A. Softer. The traction area will be slightly increased. Leading part of the tire will squee-gee the water away and prevent "aquaplaning," or riding on a film of water.

Q. What three directions will your right hand and arm operate in, simultaneously?
A. *Twistgrip*—rotary, vertical; *Handlebar*—steering, back and forth; *Front Brake*—in and out.

GLOSSARY 155

Q. What precaution is necessary after filling up at a gas station?
A. Awareness of the unstable weight (fluid) suddenly added high above the center of gravity. One U.S. gallon of fuel weighs almost 8 lbs.

Q. What is "uncontrolled" load?
A. Any load carried behind the rear wheel axle or ahead of the front wheel axle.

Q. On a wet street, is it better to use a high gear or a low gear?
A. A high gear; less torque at the traction point.

Q. Why is it difficult for a motorcycle rider to be seen in traffic?
A. A motorcyclist has small dimensions and offers poor perspective.

Q. What is the Rule of the Road?
A. Ride on the right-hand side. This rule applies in most countries of the world. There is only one Rule of the Road. Other rules are part of the highway code.

Q. Which foot supports you on the ground as you get ready to go?
A. The right (brake) foot. The left foot should be up on the footrest prepared to operate the gear lever.

Q. Which is best: (a) To be the better rider?
              (b) To have a better machine?
A. To be the better rider.

Q. Distinguish between "riding" and "driving."
A. A vehicle is driven when stability is not affected by weight of the operator. It is ridden when the operator has to maintain that stability. In the astride position rather than a sitting position, a motorcycle should be ridden, not driven.

INDEX

accessories, 115–116
acid level in battery, 118
air choke, 54
air cleaner, 116
air filter, 116
alignment, checking, 125
alternator, 117
ammeter, 117, 127
apparel for riding, 96–100
appearance of motorcycle, judging, 117–118
author's experiences, 30–33

battery, 117
 testing, 118–119
"blipping-the-throttle," 9
brake cable, 119
brake foot, 15–16, 59
brake light, 131
brake linings, 119
brake
 front, 72, 153
 rear wheel, 52, 119
brakes
 operating, 15
 testing, 119
brake-shoes, 119
braking, 71–73
 on corners, 60

cables, 118
 checking, 120, 128, 138
carburetor, 54–55
 checking, 120–121
center of gravity, 36, 37, 41–42, 45, 75, 93, 154
center-stand, 137
chain guards, 127
chains, checking, 121
changes of direction, 44–45
 see also cornering, turning
clutch, 54
 testing, 122
competition, 88
compression, testing for, 124
connecting link, 121
contact points, checking, 122
control levers, checking, 120, 123
controls
 fixed, 37–39, 47, 92, 124
 foot, 52
 handlebar, 52, 53–54, 55
cornering, 58–64
 see also turns, change of direction

decompressor, 54
design, motorcycle, 34–38

158 INDEX

dual-seats, 40–41, 92, 135

electrical switches, 55
electricity
   see alternator
      battery
      generator
      voltage regulator
engine, 153
   checking, 123–124
   size, 139
   starting, 9
engine number, 129
enjoyment of motorcycling, 19–20

face-shields, 96–98
fenders, 127
figure-eight, 16–17
fixed controls, 37–39, 47, 92, 124
foot controls, location of, 52
foot positions, 16–18, 51–53
footrest brackets, 115
footrests, 38–40, 92–93, 153
   checking, 124–125
frame, checking, 125
frame number, 129
front brake
   applying, 72, 153
   use of when mounting, 51, 52
front forks, 34, 125, 126
fuel line, 118
fuel tap, 9, 54–55, 126
fuse, checking, 126

gas tank, 54, 78
gauges, 142

gear ratio, 65
gearshift, foot, 65–68
gearshifting, 66–67
gearshift lever action, checking, 142
generator, checking, 127
gloves, 98
goggles, 96–98
guards, chain, 127

handbook, *see* manual, owner's
hand-grips, 128
handlebar controls, 52, 53–54, 55
handlebars, 75, 76, 117, 127
hand-pump, 82
hand signals, 77
headlight dimmer switch, 55–56
helmet, safety, 96, 97
horn, 55–56, 128

ignition key, 55, 131
indicator lights, 115, 117
inertia, resistance to, 43–45, 90
instruction, importance of, 20, 23
insurance, 69, 130

keys, 55, 131
kickstarter, 9, 55, 135
kinetic energy, 43–44

learning how to ride, 9–18, 49–57
license plates, 130
lights, clip-on, 117
lights, testing, 131

INDEX

locks, 56, 131
lubrication, 110, 132
luggage carrier, chrome, 115

manual, owner's, 9, 110, 132
modifications, 111–112, 133
modified seat, 117
motorcycles, practical uses for, 25–26, 28–29
 selecting new, 101–107
 selecting used, 108–143
mounting, 51
moving off, 12, 13
mud, riding through, 81–82
mufflers, 133

new motorcycle, selecting, 101–107
nuts and bolts, checking, 109, 123, 133–134

odometer, 56, 128
oil condition, *see* lubrication
oil level, checking, 142
operator's license, 130
ornaments, sharp chrome, 115, 116
over-shoe, 98
 steel, 88–89

passenger, riding with a, 78–79
posture, riding, 10–12, 74–75, 154
practice sessions, 9, 49
price, determining for resale, 134

rear suspension, 34, 125
 see also shock absorbers

registration of ownership, 129
riding
 advanced, 81–88
 basic fundamentals of, 69–80
 road test, importance of, 134–135
 rough terrain, riding through, 82–83, 86
rubbers, 135
Rule of the Road, 155
"running-in," 104–105

saddle bags, 115
sand, riding through, 82
screw slots, 123
seat
 dual, 40–41, 92, 135
 modified, 117
seating, checking, 135
seat position, 9–10, 37, 40–42, 75
servicing, 57
shields, 127
 face, 96–98
shock absorbers, 71, 136
 see also rear suspension
skids, 73–74
 avoiding, 58
spark plug, 136
spark plug lead, 118
speedometer, 128
 drive cable, 129
spokes, checking, 137
spring clip, 121
sprocket, 121, 137
stands, checking, 137–138
stator, 117
steering, 75–77
 with feet, 38–39

steering damper, 56, 76, 138
steering head, checking, 138
stony ground, riding on, 86
stoplight, 56, 131
stopping, 14–15
storage, 138–139
switches, checking, 139

tachometer, 129
taillight, 56, 131
technical advances in motorcycles, 34–35
technical data, 139
tire pressure, 45–46
tire pressure gauge, 82
tires, checking, 140–141
title, transfer of, 129
tools, 104, 142
traction point, 40, 154
traffic, riding in, 76, 78
transmission, 9, 12, 55, 65
   checking, 142
trial ride, 9–18

turns, 16–17
   see also cornering, change of direction
twistgrip, operating, 15, 51, 154

"uncontrolled" load, 155
used motorcycle, checking, 108–143

value of motorcycle, depreciation of, 134
valve cap, inner tube, 141
voltage regulator, 142–143
   see also generator

water, riding through, 83–85, 154
weight, distribution of rider's, 37–39, 41–42
wheels, checking, 143
   see also steering
wiring, checking, 143–144